VEGAN SOUPS AND STEWS

FOR ALL SEASONS

ALSO BY NAVA ATLAS

Selected cookbooks

Vegetariana (revised and updated)

Plant-Powered Protein

Vegan on a Budget

5-Ingredient Vegan

Plant Power

Wild About Greens

Vegan Holiday Kitchen

Vegan Express

The Vegetarian Family Cookbook

Great American Vegetarian (updated *American Harvest*)

...and all the previous editions of this book, including:

Vegan Soups and Hearty Stews for All Seasons

Vegetarian Soups for All Seasons

Visual nonfiction

Literary Ladies' Guide to the Writing Life

Secret Recipes for the Modern Wife

Expect the Unexpected When You're Expecting! (A Parody)

VEGAN SOUPS AND STEWS

FOR ALL SEASONS

The ultimate edition, featuring 120 recipes

NAVA ATLAS

Amberwood Press, Inc.
New York

ISBN 978-1-7371334-1-4 (paperback)
ISBN 978-1-7371334-2-1 (ebook)

Library of Congress Control Number: 2023911152

Printed in the United States

2 4 6 8 10 9 7 5 3

Interior design by Alice Atlas
Cover design by Alice Atlas & Nava Atlas
Cover photos by Hannah Kaminsky

Photos by Hannah Kaminsky, pages 15, 19, 20, 29, 34, 39, 42, 47, 48,
53, 56, 62, 65, 75, 80, 83, 84, 89, 96, 105, 106, 110, 119, 120, 127,
130, 138, 141, 144, 147, 150, 153, 163, 164, 169, 172, 177, 189, 192

CONTENTS

INTRODUCTION

Welcome to the fifth (and ultimate) edition of my collection of favorite vegan soups and stews. First published in 1992, this book has been growing and evolving ever since. From one soup lover to another, here you'll find dozens of bountiful bowlfuls for any time of year.

WE LOVE VEGAN SOUPS & STEWS!

Soups have always played a starring role in my repertoire, being one of the easiest yet most rewarding of all preparations in the kitchen. They hardly need more than basic ingredients and equipment to create a wonderfully diverse range of results.

A soup might be familiar and soothing, evoking memories of the warmth and comfort of a childhood home, or it might be a mélange of flavors that meld together in a pleasantly unexpected way. A bit less liquid and a chunkier texture results in stew—a savory and satisfying one-pot meal. Soups and stews are welcome at any time of year, reflecting the harvest of each season. Good soups and stews can:

- Showcase the tender new produce of spring or the bounty of the autumn harvest

- Brighten any humdrum winter day and soothe seasonal ailments

- Transform lush summer fruits and vegetables into refreshing chilled elixirs

The first two editions of this book were vegetarian. By the third, I had then gone vegan, and the book followed. Being vegan in the 21st century isn't much more challenging being a vegetarian. There are so many substitutions for dairy products, including an array of excellent plant-based milks and cheeses. Vegan sour cream and yogurt are much improved over their early iterations, too.

Veganism is largely about ethics—what we put on our plates reflects ideals of compassion toward all living beings and protects the environment from the ravages of animal agriculture. And bonus: A plant-based diet goes a long way toward preventing diseases caused by animal-based fare.

But veganism is also about enjoyment of great food. Vegans may meld the personal with the political on their plates, but they're also quite discerning. The myriad vegan restaurants that have sprung up everywhere feature some of the world's most creative and delicious food. And the number of gourmet and natural food companies aimed squarely at the vegan market has grown exponentially. This love for fantastic fare, prepared with compassion, is most gratifying in one's own kitchen.

It almost goes without saying that you need not be a vegan—or even a vegetarian—to enjoy these recipes. They're for anyone who appreciates fresh and flavorful seasonal produce, whole grains, healthful legumes, and plant proteins prepared with the judicious use of herbs, spices, and other seasonings. Best of all is the sense of comfort and wonderful aromas imparted by a big pot of simmering soup or stew, whetting the appetite like nothing else can.

COOKING NOTES

COOKING EQUIPMENT

The soups in this book require only the most basic kitchen equipment. Aside from a large soup pot, of course, the items needed are standard to most any kitchen: wooden spoons, a colander, a grater, measuring utensils, and good knives. And of course, a ladle for serving your lovely soups.

For the devoted soup cook, I recommend an immersion blender. This is a compact, inexpensive gadget featuring a small puree blade on the end of a wand. I find it indispensable for blending soups right in the pot — on those occasions when it's fine (or more than fine) to leave a bit of texture. All you need to do is insert the blender into the pot of soup, press the button, and blend! It's also easy to clean and easy to store.

A food processor is also useful for making grating easy and fast, while a standard or high-speed blender is useful for making super-smooth purees.

FREEZING SOUPS

Some soups freeze well, while others lose much of their flavor and texture. Thick winter bean and grain soups do pretty well, as do simple broths and stocks, but freezing often changes the texture of a smooth puree, making it more watery.

Avoid freezing soups that contain potatoes or lentils, both of which turn mushy. I don't recommend freezing soups that contain raw ingredients, which are most abundant in cold soups. The soups in this book generally don't yield large enough quantities to warrant long-term storage of leftovers. Finishing most soups while they're fresh is preferable to those that have been frozen.

TEXTURES AND CONSISTENCIES

Soup making, though essentially simple, is an inexact science. For instance, what one cook considers a large potato might seem medium-size to another, and so the amount of liquid called for in a recipe might not always yield precise results.

The soup recipes here often remind the cook to adjust the consistency or thickness, and this, like salting, should be done according to preference. Some soups (and all stews) are meant to be thick, and others brothy, but most seem to fall somewhere in between and should be tailored to your liking accordingly.

NOTES ON INGREDIENTS

BEANS: CANNED VS. COOKED FROM SCRATCH

Beans of all sorts are one of the cornerstones of plant-based soup making. They're not only a superb source of fiber and protein, but they also add great flavor and texture to soups. In the rare instances where beans are the primary ingredients of a recipe, such as in Long-Simmering Black Bean Soup (page 94), dried beans are called for. That makes both culinary and economic sense when they become the base of the soup.

In most cases where a smaller amount of cooked beans is needed, I specify both the cooked and canned quantities. It has become much easier to cook up a batch of beans if you have an Instant Pot® or a similar appliance. But many busy cooks may not want to take the time and trouble to cook a small amount of beans from scratch. By all means, if you prefer to cook beans from scratch, I won't discourage you!

That said, I vote for using canned beans rather than no beans at all. There are many varieties to be found in natural foods stores and well-stocked supermarkets, some organic. An extra advantage of organic beans is that they're less salty than commercial brands. When using canned beans of any kind, draining and rinsing them with water helps to mitigate the sodium factor.

PLANT-BASED MILK

How things have changed in the world of plant-based dairy since I first published this book as *Soups for All Seasons* in 1992! Back then, the book (and I) were vegetarian, and so the choices presented in ingredient lists were "low-fat milk and soy milk." When the book first went vegan (as I did), the choice became "rice milk or soy milk." Neither are ideal for soups, but that's all we had at the time.

Now, there is a plethora of good choices when it comes to plant-based milks made from oats, almonds, cashews, hemp, and more. The ingredients in this edition specify "unsweetened plant-based milk," allowing you to choose your favorite. My favorite for soups is oat milk.

VEGAN CHEESES

This is a niche that has really exploded in the last couple of decades. Most supermarkets carry an array of brands to choose from, and it's up to you to use your favorite. Shreds are most common form of vegan cheese called for in these recipes, because they add a bit of cheesy deliciousness to certain soups.

VEGAN SOUR CREAM AND YOGURT

Like plant-based milks and cheeses, vegan sour cream and yogurt have improved greatly over the years. Some brands of vegan sour cream rely on natural ingredients, while others are filled with additives, so read labels and opt for the former. As for vegan yogurt, my favorites are cashew and coconut yogurts. There are other delicious type of plant-based yogurt, too—and even soy yogurt has come a long way.

In these recipes, vegan sour cream or yogurt are most often used as a garnish to dollop onto soups when serving. Occasionally they're used as base ingredients, especially in cold soups.

If you're the DIY type, you can still make your own silken tofu-based sour cream (both this and the packaged option are given in the recipes). Here's a simple how-to:

Homemade vegan sour cream: Combine a 12.3-ounce package of extra-firm silken tofu, 2 to 3 tablespoons unsweetened plant-based milk (as needed), 1 tablespoon lemon juice (or to taste), and ¼ teaspoon salt in a food processor. Process until very smoothly pureed, then transfer to a container with an airtight lid. This keeps well for 3 to 4 days, refrigerated.

OILS AND VEGAN BUTTER

As you'll soon see, my oil of choice in most soups is olive oil, and even that is used sparingly. Unless extra-virgin is specified for its more assertive flavor, you can use any kind of olive oil. Are you on an oil-free diet? Skip the oil and use a bit of broth to sweat onions, garlic, and the like in steps calling for a sauté.

On occasion, I call for vegan butter. There are so many brands available that I'll forego giving a specific recommendation. The one caveat is to avoid vegan butters based on palm oil, because its cultivation and harvesting is harmful to the environment and native species.

SEASONING BLENDS

The success of a meatless soup depends primarily on the flavor and freshness of its main ingredients, and next, on using a variety of seasonings and flavorings. Dried seasonings are added early in the cooking process; fresh herbs are best added at the very end.

Quantities of seasonings given in soup recipes—in this book or others—should be tailored to individual tastes. As a perennial soup enthusiast, I have always loved to experiment with a pinch of this spice, a quarter teaspoon of this herb, and a half teaspoon of that. It's all part of the fun and artistry of making soup. That said, a favorite time-saver I've adopted through the years has been to use seasoning blends like Italian herb or the salt-free all-purpose varieties. There are many excellent natural brands—even organic options. They're readily available, tasty, and convenient.

Small quantities of certain seasoning blends contribute to the zesty flavor needed to make any soup taste great. Feel free to experiment with the many varieties available. Here are the seasoning blends I use most often in making soups:

CURRY POWDER A good curry powder should be fragrant and pungent. Different blends possess varying amounts of heat; how much is entirely up to your preference for hot vs. mild spicing. You can find the best blends in Indian groceries if there's one near you.

ITALIAN SEASONING A blend of several herbs such as oregano, thyme, marjoram, and rosemary, this is commonly available at specialty groceries as well as most supermarkets.

SALT-FREE SEASONING This savory blend of herbs and spices is an instant flavor booster for many types of soups. There are several good brands available in supermarkets and natural food stores. My favorites from the supermarket are Mrs. Dash Table Blend® and McCormick Perfect Pinch®. From the natural food store, Spike® is a great product, as is Frontier All-Purpose Seasoning®. There are other good brands (including store brands); experiment with them and make use of whichever you prefer. As long as they contain a lots of herbs and spices, but no salt, you're good to go.

A few more tried-and-true tips for seasoning soups and stews:

- Add salt toward the end of cooking time to give the other flavors a chance to develop and to avoid over-salting. Salt a little at a time, stir it in thoroughly, and taste frequently.

- Those who need to limit their intake of salt might try adding lemon juice or more herbs and spices than called for.

- Add extra zest and heat to soups with ginger. Fresh ginger can sometimes be frustratingly dry and stringy, even when it looks fine on the outside. I prefer minced ginger that comes in a jar or squeeze bottle. It's finely and evenly minced, moist, and fresh tasting—perfect for soup and so convenient.

- Most importantly, use the amount of seasoning given here as a guide. Use more or less to suit your own taste and the palates of those to whom you will be serving soups and stews.

SOUP STARTERS FOR EXTRA FLAVOR

Contrary to culinary myth, the absence of a strong-flavored meat broth doesn't present a huge challenge to making great soups and stews. Many ethnic cuisines produce classic soups that in their original form are completely vegetarian or vegan. True, almost any soup can benefit from a good broth to boost flavor, but fresh and flavorful ingredients and judicious seasoning are even more crucial to a soup's success.

In this book's soup recipes, I often list an amount of water needed plus a vegetable bouillon cube or two, as that's the simplest shortcut. With all the fresh ingredients and flavorings in the soups, this is generally sufficient. Occasionally, especially for brothy Asian soups, a 32-ounce carton of vegetable broth is my first choice. There are many all-natural and even organic brands of these kinds of soup starters. Here are a few options for creating a good soup base:

HOMEMADE VEGETABLE BROTH

If you're a fan of DIY, you may enjoy making broth from scratch. You'll need to allow at least an extra hour before making the actual soup to prepare and cook this stock. Or, you can do so a day ahead of time. Truth be told, I no longer do this, and I don't expect you to, either. But there will be some people who prefer making their own broth, so a basic recipe is provided on page 11.

VEGETABLE BOUILLON CUBES

This is the easiest and most economical option. Look for a no-salt added brand that's completely vegan. My favorite is Rapunzel® Vegan Vegetable Bouillon. It's packed with flavor, organic, and has a salt-free option. Each cube is actually equivalent to two standard-sized cubes.

VEGETABLE BROTH POWDER

A tablespoon of this type of stock enhancer goes a long way in a pot of soup. However, I don't recommend it in the ingredients listings, as it's more difficult to find a low-sodium variety of this product than either bouillon cubes or prepared broths. However, if you come across a low-salt brand with all-natural ingredients, give it a try.

PREPARED VEGETABLE BROTH

I occasionally call for this product for brothy soups, as you'll see in the recipes. It comes in 32-ounce aseptic cartons; choose low-sodium if you prefer. I usually keep a couple cartons in the pantry, where they keep at room temperature almost indefinitely.

BASIC VEGETABLE BROTH

For the true DIY soup cook   Makes about 6 cups

This is a basic stock that may be used in place of water in almost any savory soup or stew for added depth of flavor. It's also a good way to use up vegetables that are limp or less than perfectly fresh. I'm not going to kid myself that most readers will choose a soup to make and then backtrack to make a broth. But true purists, or those who have a few stray vegetables in the crisper that need to be used up, may find this recipe useful.

7 cups water
1 large onion, chopped
2 to 3 cloves garlic, minced
2 to 3 medium carrots, sliced
2 large celery stalks, sliced
1 medium potato or sweet potato,
  scrubbed and diced
1 to 2 cups coarsely chopped vegetables
  of your choice (green cabbage, leeks,
  peppers, zucchini, etc.)
2 teaspoons salt-free seasoning
  (see page 8 for brands)

1 Combine all the ingredients in a large soup pot. Bring to a slow boil, then lower the heat. Simmer gently over low heat with the cover ajar for 40 to 45 minutes.

2 Strain the broth through a fine mesh strainer. Discard the solids or puree them well and stir them into the broth for a thicker consistency.

ONION & GARLIC BROTH

A homemade broth with depth   Makes about 6 cups

This broth may be used as an extra-flavorful soup starter or as an extra-flavorful alternative to Basic Vegetable Broth (page 11). It's also quite soothing for colds and other cold-season ailments.

1 tablespoon olive oil
1 large onion, chopped, or 2 medium leeks,
**   white parts only, chopped and well rinsed**
4 to 6 cloves garlic, minced
¼ cup dry red wine, optional
6 cups water

1 Heat the oil in a 2-quart saucepan or small soup pot. Add the onion or leeks and sauté over medium heat until golden.

2 Add the garlic and continue to sauté until the onion or leeks brown lightly.

3 Add the optional wine and water. Bring to a slow boil, then lower the heat. Simmer gently over low heat with the cover ajar for 40 to 45 minutes.

4 You may leave the onions and garlic in, if you wish, or strain the broth through a fine strainer. Discard the solids or puree them and add to soup for a thicker consistency.

SIMPLE MISO BROTH

The Japanse classic, so easy to make at home   Makes about 6 cups

---

Miso is a nutritious, high-protein paste fermented from soybeans and salt (or a combination of soybeans, grains, and salt). There's also a new iteration — chickpea miso, which is great for those who need to avoid soy. Miso is available in natural foods stores and Asian groceries, where you can also find the sea vegetable kombu. Pungent-tasting miso is most commonly used to make simple broths like this one. Note that once the miso is stirred into water it shouldn't be boiled, to preserve its beneficial enzymes.

1 recipe Basic Vegetable Broth (page 11)
  or a 32-ounce container low-sodium
  vegetable broth plus 2 cups water
2 strips kombu, each about 3 by 5 inches
2 to 4 tablespoons miso, to taste

1 Combine the broth with the kombu in a 2-quart saucepan or small soup pot and bring to a slow boil.

2 Dissolve the desired amount of miso in just enough warm water to make it pourable. Stir into the broth and remove from the heat.

3 Let stand for 30 minutes, if time allows, or serve at once. Either way, remove and discard the kombu just before serving.

VARIATIONS Embellish miso broth with any of the following: diced tofu; cooked Asian noodles; thinly sliced scallion; grated fresh daikon radish or white turnip; crisp cucumber, seeded and grated.

DRIED SHIITAKE MUSHROOM BROTH

A sublime soup starter or a base for a simple soup   Makes about 6 cups

This easy dried shiitake mushroom broth is a richly flavored boost for Asian-inspired vegetable and noodle soups. It's also pleasing eaten as is, embellished with the optional ingredients listed below. Fresh shiitakes are delicious, of course, but in dried form their flavor is more intense, perfect for making a quick broth.

2 teaspoons neutral vegetable oil
1 small onion, finely chopped
1 to 2 cloves garlic, minced
32-ounce carton vegetable broth
   plus 2 cups water or 6 cups water
   with 2 vegetable bouillon cubes
8 to 10 dried shiitake mushrooms
1 to 2 tablespoons soy sauce
   or tamari, to taste

Optional embellishments (choose 2 or 3)
Diced tofu
Cooked Asian noodles
Thinly sliced scallion
Grated fresh daikon radish or turnip
Crisp cucumber, quartered, seeds cut
   away, and sliced or cut into matchsticks

1 Heat the oil in a 2-quart saucepan or small soup pot. Add the onion and garlic and sauté over low heat until golden.

2 Add the broth, mushrooms, and soy sauce. Bring to a slow boil, then lower the heat. Simmer gently over low heat with the cover ajar for 15 minutes.

3 Remove from the heat and let stand for 15 minutes longer. Strain through a sieve, reserving the mushrooms. Trim and discard the tough stems. Slice the caps and return them to the broth.

4 Use the broth as a starter for Asian-style soups or gravy, or embellish simply with any of the items suggested in the ingredient list and serve immediately.

SCALLION PANCAKES

Simple to make and even easier to eat   Makes about 8

These delectable pancakes are appreciated by adults and children alike, and fantastic served with Asian-inspired soups.

2 cups flour (see options)
1 teaspoon salt
½ teaspoon baking powder
2 cups water
1 ½ cups thinly sliced scallions
2 tablespoons sesame seeds, optional
Neutral vegetable oil, as needed

1 Combine the flour, salt, and baking powder in a large mixing bowl and stir together.

2 Make a well in the center of the flour mixture and pour in the water. Whisk together until smooth, then stir in the scallion and optional sesame seeds.

3 Lightly oil a 6- to 7-inch nonstick skillet and let it get nice and hot. Ladle the batter onto it in ¾-cup portions, or enough to cover the surface evenly. Cook over medium-high heat on both sides until golden brown.

4 Transfer the first pancake to a paper towel-lined plate. Cover it with another layer of paper towel. Repeat with the remaining batter. To serve, cut each pancake into 4 wedges.

FLOUR OPTIONS For wheat-based flours, choose from among light spelt, white whole wheat, einkorn, or whole wheat pastry flour. Use a combination of these flours, if you'd like. For gluten-free flours, you can use a GF flour blend (like Bob's Red Mill) or sorghum flour.

QUICK SUNFLOWER CHEESE BREAD

An easy, cheesy loaf

This tasty bread goes well with many soups. Try it with tomato-based and bean soups.

2 cups light spelt or whole
   wheat pastry flour
1 ½ teaspoons baking powder
1 teaspoon baking soda
½ teaspoon salt
1 cup plain plant-based yogurt
2 tablespoons safflower oil
1 tablespoon maple syrup or agave nectar
2 teaspoons prepared mustard
¼ cup plant-based milk, or more as needed
1 cup firmly packed cheddar-
   style vegan cheese shreds
¼ cup toasted sunflower seeds

1   Preheat the oven to 350° F.

2   Combine the first 4 (dry) ingredients in a mixing bowl and stir together.

3   In another bowl, combine the yogurt, oil, syrup, mustard, and ¼ cup of the plant-based milk. Whisk together until well blended.

4   Make a well in the dry ingredients and pour in the wet mixture. Stir until well combined, adding more plant-based milk as needed to make a smooth, slightly stiff batter.

5   Fold in the cheese and half of the sunflower seeds.

6   Spoon the batter into a lightly oiled 9-by-5-by-3-inch loaf pan (if you'd like, cut and fit a piece of parchment into the bottom of the pan for easier removal of the loaf once baked and cooled). Sprinkle the remaining sunflower seeds over the top.

7   Bake for 45 minutes, or until the top is golden brown and crusty. When the loaf pan is cool enough to handle, remove the loaf, place it on a rack, and allow it to cool to room temperature or until just warm before slicing.

CHEESE & HERB CORN MUFFINS

Delicious little herb-flavored breads

Moist and flavorful, these tasty vegan cheese and herb corn muffins pair perfectly with hearty soups. I especially like them with bean soups and chili, as a change of pace from pan cornbread. Fresh herbs add visual interest as well as flavor.

1 cup stone ground cornmeal

1 cup whole wheat pastry flour

1 teaspoon baking powder

½ teaspoon baking soda

½ teaspoon salt

1 cup unsweetened applesauce

¼ cup olive oil

⅓ cup unsweetened plant-based milk, or more, as needed

1 cup vegan cheddar-style cheese shreds

½ cup chopped fresh parsley or cilantro

2 to 3 scallions, thinly sliced, or ¼ cup chopped chives

½ cup cooked fresh or thawed frozen corn kernels, optional

1   Preheat the oven to 400° F.

2   Combine the first 5 (dry) ingredients in a mixing bowl and stir together.

3   Make a well in the center of the dry ingredients. Pour in the applesauce, oil, and plant-based milk. Stir until well combined, adding more nondairy milk as needed to make a smooth, slightly stiff batter. Don't be tempted to add too much or the muffins won't bake through. Add just enough to moisten all the dry ingredients.

4   Fold in the cheese shreds, parsley, scallions, and optional corn kernels.

5   Divide the batter among 12 paper-lined muffin tins. Bake for 20 to 25 minutes, or until the muffin tops are golden brown and a toothpick or knife inserted into the center of one tests clean.

6   Cool on a rack or plate. Store leftover muffins in an airtight container once completely cooled.

FOCACCIA BREAD

An earthy whole wheat flatbread

Although this traditional Italian bread is yeasted, it doesn't take as long to make as other yeasted breads; it only requires one rather brief rising. If you're making a long-simmering soup, this bread will likely fit into the time frame. It's a natural pairing with Italian-style soups like Minestrone (page 70), but is good with almost any tomato-based soup.

1 package active dry yeast
1 cup warm water
1 tablespoon natural granulated sugar
¼ cup extra-virgin olive oil
1 ½ cups whole wheat bread flour
1 cup unbleached white flour
1 teaspoon salt
1 tablespoon minced fresh garlic, optional
Coarse salt
Dried oregano or rosemary

1   Pour the yeast into the warm water and let stand to dissolve for 5 to 10 minutes. Stir in the sugar and two tablespoons of the oil.

2   In a large mixing bowl, combine the flours and salt. Work in the yeast mixture using your hands, then turn the dough out onto a well-floured board. Knead for 5 minutes, adding additional flour if the dough is too sticky. Shape into a round and roll out into a circle with a 12-inch diameter.

3   Place the dough on an oiled and floured baking sheet, cover with a tea towel, and let rise in a warm place for 30 to 40 minutes.

4   Preheat the oven to 400° F.

5   When the dough has finished rising, poke shallow holes into its surface with your fingers, at even intervals. Sprinkle the remaining 2 tablespoons of olive oil over the top evenly, followed by the optional garlic, coarse salt, and herbs.

6   Bake for 20 to 25 minutes, or until the bread is golden on top and sounds hollow when tapped. Serve warm, cut into wedges, or invite everyone break off pieces.

GREEN CHILI CORNBREAD

Studded with jalapeños and corn   Makes 9 squares

This moist cornbread is an ideal companion for bean soups and chilis.

1 ½ cups stone ground cornmeal
½ cup unbleached white flour
¼ cup toasted wheat germ
1 teaspoon baking soda
½ teaspoon baking powder
1 teaspoon salt
1 cup plain vegan yogurt
2 tablespoons olive oil
2 tablespoons plant-based milk,
   plus more as needed
1 to 2 fresh jalapeño peppers, seeded
   and minced, or a 4-ounce can
   chopped mild green chilis
½ cup frozen corn kernels, thawed

1   Preheat the oven to 400° F.

2   Combine the first 6 (dry) ingredients in a mixing bowl and stir together.

3   Make a well in the center of the dry ingredients. Pour in the yogurt, oil, and half of the plant-based milk. Stir until well combined, adding more plant-based milk as needed to make a smooth, slightly stiff batter.

4   Stir in the jalapeños and corn kernels into the batter.

5   Spoon the mixture into an oiled 8- or 9-inch square baking pan. Bake for 20 to 25 minutes, or until the top is golden and a knife inserted in the center tests clean. Let cool slightly; cut into squares and serve warm.

A TRIO OF SIMPLE ACCOMPANIMENTS

BRUSCHETTA

These garlicky toasts are great companions for just about any type of soup (other than fruit soups). Cut as many ¾-inch-thick slices as you need from a long Italian bread — so much the better if it's whole grain. Arrange the slices on a baking sheet. Bake in a preheated 350° F oven for 10 to 15 minutes, turning once, or until both sides are golden and crisp. Watch them carefully!

Remove the toasts from the oven. When cool enough to handle, rub one side of each toast with an open side of a clove of garlic that has been cut in half lengthwise. If desired, brush a bit of olive oil on one side of each of the toasts as well.

GARLIC CROUTONS

These croutons are so easy to make, and are also a good way to use up bread that may otherwise go stale. Use ends and pieces of whole grain bread, allowing about 1 small slice per serving. Rub each piece of bread gently on one or both sides with the open side of a garlic clove that has been cut in half lengthwise. Cut the bread into approximately ½-inch dice.

Prepare the croutons in one of the two following ways: Arrange them on a baking sheet and bake in a 275° F oven for 20 minutes or so, until dry and crisp. Or, simply toast the croutons in a heavy skillet over medium heat, stirring frequently, about 20 minutes, or until dry and crisp. Allow the croutons to cool on a plate. They may be used as soon as they have cooled, but if you can leave them out at room temperature for at least 30 minutes or so, they stay crisper when added to soup.

CRISPY TORTILLA STRIPS

Crispy fried corn tortilla strips are a fun topping for Southwestern-style soups and stews. Allow for ½ of a good-quality corn tortilla per serving, or a bit more, if anyone wants to replenish as the soup is eaten.

Cut each tortilla into approximately ½ by 2-inch strips. Heat a large skillet (coat with a little cooking oil spray or a little olive oil) and add tortilla strips in a single layer (don't crowd the skillet; do this in batches). Toast the tortilla strips in the skillet over medium-high heat, turning frequently, until dry and crisp, then remove to a plate to cool.

FALL

Autumn is an inviting time to make soup. In early to mid-season, the rich colors and lively flavors of the harvest can be shown off to great advantage in a warming bowl of soup. Later in the season, serving a tasty bowl of soup or stew is a heartwarming way to temper the effects of chilly weather.

FRENCH ONION SOUP

A vegan take on the classic, with bread and melted cheese   6 servings

Vegan French onion soup is a plant-based spin on the classic, complete with crusty bread and melted vegan cheese. The traditional recipe uses a non-vegan broth; the plant-based swap-in is dark miso or a vegetable bouillon base. Just a small amount of either of these flavor-packed ingredients gives the broth a robust flavor and eliminates the need for further salting.

2 tablespoons olive oil

8 medium yellow onions,
   quartered and thinly sliced

2 cloves garlic, minced

6 cups water

¼ cup dry red wine, optional

2 tablespoons dark miso or vegan
   bouillon base, or more, to taste

Freshly ground pepper to taste

¼ cup chopped fresh parsley, optional

1 French baguette or narrow
   loaf Italian bread

1 ½ cups mozzarella-style vegan
   cheese shreds, or as needed

1   Heat the oil in a soup pot. Add the onions and sauté over medium-low heat until golden. Add the garlic and continue to sauté slowly until the onions are lightly and evenly browned, stirring frequently, about 20 to 25 minutes.

2   Pour the water over the onions and give them a good stir. Add the optional wine and bring to a slow boil, then lower the heat. Simmer gently over low heat with the cover ajar for 15 minutes.

3   If using miso, dissolve it in a little warm water in a cup to make it pourable. Add to the soup to taste. Or, if using bouillon base, add to the soup to taste. Season with pepper and stir in the parsley, if using.

4   While the soup is cooking, preheat the oven to 375° F.

5   Cut the bread into 1-inch-thick slices on a slight diagonal, allowing 2 slices per serving. Arrange on a parchment-lined baking sheet. Bake for 15 minutes, or until dry and crisp, turning the slices over once about halfway through the baking time.

6   Sprinkle the baked bread slices with a generous amount of cheese, and return to the oven until melted.

7   Ladle the soup out into shallow bowls. Arrange 2 slices of the bread on top. Serve at once.

CREAM OF WHITE VEGETABLES

Pureed potatoes, white onions, and turnips, with a colorful garnish   8 servings

With a super-smooth pureed base, this soup is comfort and simplicity in a bowl. If you can, use the big, pure white onions that are abundant in the fall.

2 tablespoons olive oil
1 ½ pounds white onions (if unavailable, substitute yellow onions)
1 ½ pounds white turnips, peeled and diced
3 large potatoes, peeled and diced
2 to 3 cloves garlic, minced
½ cup unsweetened plant-based milk, or more, as needed
Salt and freshly ground pepper to taste

Garnish
1 teaspoon olive oil
1 large red bell pepper, finely diced
½ cup frozen green peas, thawed
3 scallions, thinly sliced
¼ to ½ cup chopped fresh parsley

1   Heat the oil in a soup pot. Add the onions and sauté over medium-low heat, covered. Stir occasionally for about 15 minutes, or until golden.

2   Set aside 1 cup of the turnip dice. Add the remaining turnips to the soup pot, followed by the potatoes and garlic. Add enough water to cover all but about ½ inch of the vegetables. Bring to a slow boil, then lower the heat. Simmer gently over low heat with the cover ajar until the vegetables are tender, about 30 to 40 minutes.

3   Use a slotted spoon to transfer the vegetables to a food processor or blender and puree in batches, then transfer back to the soup pot. Or, skip the food processor and insert an immersion blender into the pot and blend the soup until pureed to your liking.

4   Stir in enough plant-based milk to give the soup a thick but fluid consistency. Season with salt and pepper. Reheat very gently while preparing garnish.

5   *For the garnish:* Heat the oil in a medium-sized skillet. Add the bell pepper, reserved turnip dice, and about 2 tablespoons of water. Cover and sweat over medium heat until tender-crisp, about 7 minutes. Add the peas, scallions, and parsley, and cook, covered, about 5 minutes longer, adding a bit more water if needed to keep the skillet moist.

6   Ladle the soup into bowls and divide the garnish among them, arranging it in the center of each bowl.

NEW ENGLAND CLAM-LESS CHOWDER

A mélange of potatoes and fresh corn, minus the seafood   6 to 8 servings

*Baked tofu is an excellent stand-in for the
seafood in this classic American soup. Serving
it with tiny oyster crackers (which are basi-
cally saltines) adds a traditional, fun touch.*

2 tablespoons olive oil
1 large onion, finely chopped
2 celery stalks, finely diced
2 tablespoons unbleached white flour
4 cups water
2 vegetable bouillon cubes
4 medium potatoes, scrubbed and diced
3 cups thawed frozen or cooked fresh
   corn kernels (from 3 to 4 ears)
1 teaspoon salt-free seasoning
   (see page 8 for brands)
1 teaspoon ground cumin
4 ounces (about ½ package)
   baked tofu, finely diced
2 cups unsweetened plant-based
   milk, or more, as needed
Salt and freshly ground pepper to taste
Oyster crackers for serving, optional

1   Heat the oil in a soup pot. Add the onion and
celery and sauté over medium-low heat until both
are golden, about 8 to 10 minutes.

2   Sprinkle the flour over the onion and celery, a little at a time, and stir in. Slowly stir in the water, then
add the bouillon cubes, potatoes, corn, seasoning,
and cumin. Bring to a slow boil, then lower the heat.
Simmer gently over low heat with the cover ajar until the potatoes are tender, about 20 to 25 minutes.

3   With the back of a wooden spoon, mash a small
amount of the potatoes to thicken the base. Stir in
the baked tofu, then add plant-based milk as needed. The soup should be somewhat thick but not
overly dense.

4   Return to a gentle simmer, then season with salt
and pepper. If time allows, let the soup stand off the
heat for an hour or two, then heat through before
serving. Pass around oyster crackers for topping individual servings, if you'd like.

POTATO, CHEESE & GREEN CHILI SOUP

A contemporary classic from the American Southwest   6 to 8 servings

---

Here's a great soup to make in the early fall, while fresh corn and tomatoes are still available. Use jalapeños for a spicier soup; poblanos are nice and mild. Serve with Crispy Tortilla Strips (page 25) as a festive garnish.

1 tablespoon olive oil
1 large onion, chopped
2 to 3 cloves garlic, minced
1 large green bell pepper, finely chopped
5 medium potatoes, peeled and diced
6 cups water
2 vegetable bouillon cubes
1 cup chopped fresh ripe tomatoes
1 cup cooked fresh or thawed
   frozen corn kernels
2 fresh jalapeño peppers, seeded
   and minced, or 2 poblano peppers,
   seeded and finely chopped
2 teaspoons cumin
1 ½ cups vegan cheddar or jack-
   style cheese shreds
1 cup unsweetened plant-based
   milk or more, as needed
Salt and freshly ground pepper to taste

1   Heat the oil in a soup pot. Add the onion and sauté over medium-low heat until translucent. Add the garlic and green pepper and sauté until the mixture begins to brown lightly.

2   Add the potatoes, water, and bouillon cubes. Bring to a slow boil, then lower the heat. Simmer gently over low heat with the cover ajar until the potatoes are just tender, about 15 minutes.

3   Coarsely mash about half of the potatoes in the pot with a potato masher.

4   Stir in the tomatoes, corn, chili peppers, and cumin, and simmer gently for 15 minutes longer, stirring occasionally.

5   Sprinkle in the cheese, a little at a time, stirring it until fairly well melted. Add enough plant-based milk to give the soup a thick yet flowing consistency.

6   Season with salt and pepper and continue to simmer over very low heat for 5 minutes longer. If time allows, let the soup stand off the heat for an hour or so. Reheat before serving. Adjust the consistency with more plant-based milk, if the soup becomes too thick, then taste to adjust the seasonings.

GOLDEN POTATO SOUP

With roasted garlic and red peppers, with a hint of apple   6 to 8 servings

Though this soup is low in fat, the buttery flavor of golden potatoes makes it taste rich and luscious. Roasted fresh garlic and jarred red peppers add a deep smoky flavor, and a hint of apple mellows it all out.

1 large or 2 medium whole heads garlic
1 tablespoon olive oil
1 large or two medium onions,
    finely chopped
6 to 7 medium golden potatoes,
    peeled and diced
1 medium tender apple (such as Cortland
    or Golden Delicious), peeled and diced
¼ cup dry white wine, optional
3 to 4 scallions, thinly sliced
6-ounce jar roasted red bell peppers,
    drained and cut into ½-inch squares
1 to 1 ½ cups unsweetened plant-
    based milk, or as needed
Salt and freshly ground pepper to taste

1 Preheat the oven to 350° F, or a toaster oven to 375° F. Place the whole garlic heads on a baking sheet and bake for 40 minutes.

2 Heat the oil in a soup pot. Add the onions and sauté over medium-low heat until golden. Add the potatoes, apple, optional wine, and just enough water to cover. Bring to a slow boil, then lower the heat. Simmer gently over low heat with the cover ajar for 25 to 30 minutes, or until the potato is quite tender.

3 When the garlic is done, squeeze the soft pulp from the cloves right into the soup and discard the skins. Mash the potatoes in the pot with a potato masher until the base is thick and chunky.

4 Add the scallions, roasted peppers, and enough plant-based milk to give the soup a thick consistency. Simmer gently for 5 minutes longer. Season with salt and pepper.

5 If time allows, let the soup stand off the heat for an hour. Before serving, heat through very gently. Adjust the consistency with more plant-based milk as needed, then taste to adjust the seasonings.

MELLOW SWEET POTATO SOUP

Subtly spiced, with a colorful garnish

This warming soup tempts the eye with an appealing golden color and pleases the palate with the delectable flavor of sweet potatoes.

2 tablespoons olive oil
2 medium onions, chopped
2 medium carrots, peeled and diced
1 large celery stalk, diced
A handful of celery leaves
3 to 4 medium-large sweet potatoes
    peeled and diced (about 6 cups)
1 teaspoon ground cumin
½ teaspoon dried thyme
¼ teaspoon ground nutmeg
1 ½ cups unsweetened plant-
    based milk, or as needed
Juice of ½ lime (slice the other
    half thinly for garnish)
Salt and freshly ground pepper to taste

Topping
1 tablespoon olive oil
6 kale leaves, preferably lacinato,
    stemmed and thinly sliced
1 ½ cups fresh or frozen
    (thawed) corn kernels
2 scallions, thinly sliced
¼ cup cilantro leaves

1 Heat the oil in a soup pot. Add the onions, carrots, and celery, and sauté over medium-low heat until all are golden.

2 Add the celery leaves and sweet potato dice. Add just enough water to cover all but about an inch of the vegetables. Bring to a slow boil. Stir in the cumin, thyme, and nutmeg, then lower the heat. Simmer gently over low heat with the cover ajar until the sweet potatoes and vegetables are tender, about 20 to 25 minutes.

3 Transfer the solid ingredients to a food processor or blender with about 1 cup of the cooking liquid. Process until smoothly pureed (or leave a bit chunky), then stir back into the soup pot. Or, skip the food processor and insert an immersion blender into the pot and blend the soup until pureed to your liking.

4 Add enough plant-based milk to give the soup a slightly thick consistency. Stir in the lime juice and season with salt and pepper. Simmer over low heat for 10 minutes longer.

5 For the topping, heat the oil in a medium skillet. Add the kale and sauté until wilted, about 2 to 3 minutes. Add the corn and sauté for 2 to 3 minutes longer. Add the scallions and continue to sauté for another minute. Stir in the cilantro and remove from the heat. Mound a little of this topping mixture on each serving of soup, along with a thin slice or two of fresh lime.

CREAMY MIXED MUSHROOM SOUP

A feast of fungi in a smooth protein puree

This flavorful soup gets its creaminess from a base of pureed white beans, silken tofu, and plant-based milk. It's a soothing segue into the the cooler seasons.

2 tablespoons olive oil

1 large onion, chopped

2 to 3 cloves garlic, minced

2 medium potatoes, peeled and diced

2 large celery stalks, with leaves, diced

32-ounce carton vegetable broth

½ teaspoon dried basil

½ teaspoon dried thyme

¼ cup dry white wine, optional

12 ounces cremini mushrooms, stemmed, cleaned, and sliced

4 to 6 ounces fresh shiitake mushrooms, stemmed and sliced

15-ounce can white beans (cannellini), drained and rinsed

12.3-ounce package firm silken tofu, coarsely crumbled

2 cups unsweetened plant-based milk, or more, as needed

Salt and freshly ground pepper to taste

½ cup minced fresh parsley for garnish

1 Heat the oil in a large soup pot. Add the onion and sauté over medium-low heat until translucent. Add the garlic and continue to sauté until both are golden.

2 Add potatoes, celery stalks and leaves, broth, basil, thyme, and optional wine. Bring to a slow boil, then lower the heat. Simmer gently over low heat with the cover ajar for 15 to 20 minutes, or until the vegetables are tender.

3 Meanwhile, combne the cremini and shiitake mushrooms in a small skillet or saucepan with just enough water to keep them moist. Cover and cook over medium heat for 10 minutes.

4 Stir the beans and tofu into the soup pot. Puree the mixture in batches in a food processor or blender, then return to the soup pot. Or, skip the food processor and insert an immersion blender into the pot and blend the soup until pureed to your liking.

5 Stir the cooked mushrooms into the soup along with enough plant-based milk to give it a slightly thick consistency. Season with salt and pepper. If time allows, let the soup stand for an hour or two, though you can serve it right away if you can't wait.

6 If you've let the soup stand, heat through before serving and adjust the consistency with more plant-based milk, if too thick; adjust the seasonings as well. After ladling the soup into bowls, sprinkle each serving with a little parsley.

CREAMY POTATO SQUASH SOUP

A heavenly puree of hardy fall vegetables   6 to 8 servings

Onions, garlic, winter squash, and silken tofu meld with the familiar flavor of potatoes, making this a wonderful vehicle for getting several nourishing ingredients into very young or fussy eaters.

1 medium acorn or golden acorn
   squash, about 1 pound
1 tablespoon olive oil
1 large onion, chopped
2 to 3 cloves garlic, minced
4 medium-large potatoes (about
   1 ½ pounds), peeled and diced
2 vegetable bouillon cubes
½ teaspoon curry powder
½ teaspoon dried dill
12.3-ounce package firm or extra-firm
   silken tofu, coarsely crumbled
2 cups unsweetened plant-based
   milk, or as needed
Salt and freshly ground pepper to taste
Minced fresh parsley for garnish, optional

1 Place the squash in a microwave-safe container. Microwave for 6 to 8 minutes, until it can be easily pierced with a knife. Or, if using the oven for other foods, you can bake the squash in the oven. Wrap in foil and place in a small baking dish. Bake at 375° F or 400° F for 30 to 45 minutes, or until tender.

2 Let the squash cool until it can be easily handled. Split it in half, remove the seeds and fibers, and scoop the flesh away from the skin. Set aside until needed.

3 Heat the oil in a soup pot. Add the onion and sauté over medium-low heat until golden.

4 Add the garlic, potatoes, bouillon cubes, curry powder, and dill. Add enough water to just cover the ingredients. Bring to a slow boil, then lower the heat. Simmer gently over low heat with the cover ajar until the potatoes are tender, about 25 minutes.

5 Add the baked squash, tofu, and plant-based milk. Transfer the solid ingredients to a food processor or blender (in batches, if need be) and process until smoothly pureed. Add a little of the plant-based milk to each batch. Return the puree to the pot and stir in. Or, skip the food processor and insert an immersion blender into the pot and blend the soup until pureed to your liking.

6 If need be, add more plant-based milk to give the soup a slightly thick consistency. Simmer gently until piping hot. Season with salt and pepper and serve.

CURRIED RED LENTIL SOUP

With sweet potatoes and chard or other greens   6 servings

Red lentils, which cook to a warm golden color, are available in natural food stores and well-stocked supermarkets. Serve this nourishing and satisfying thick soup with fresh flatbread.

2 tablespoons olive oil

1 cup chopped red or yellow onion

2 to 3 cloves garlic, minced

6 cups water

1 ½ cups dried red lentils, rinsed

2 large or 3 medium sweet
   potatoes, peeled and diced

1 teaspoon grated fresh or bottled ginger

2 teaspoons good-quality curry
   powder, or to taste

½ teaspoon ground coriander and/or cumin

¼ teaspoon cinnamon

¼ teaspoon ground nutmeg

6 to 8 ounces chard (Swiss, green, or
   rainbow), or swap in mustard greens,
   escarole, or 5 ounces baby spinach)

Juice of 1 lemon or lime

Salt and freshly ground pepper to taste

1 Heat the oil in a soup pot. Add the onion and sauté over medium-low heat until translucent. Add the garlic and continue to sauté until both are golden.

2 Add the water, followed by the lentils, sweet potatoes, and seasonings. Bring to a slow boil, then lower the heat. Simmer gently over low heat with the cover ajarr until the lentils are mushy and the sweet potatoes are done, about 20 to 25 minutes.

3 Meanwhile, if using chard, cut leaves away from midribs; slice leaves into narrow shreds; slice midribs thinly if you'd like to use them. For mustard greens or escarole, cut into bite-size pieces, stems and all. Rinse the greens very well. Baby spinach needs no prep. Stir greens into the soup along with the lemon juice. If the soup is too thick, adjust the consistency with a small amount of water.

4 Continue to simmer gently until the greens are just done. All of them cook quickly, especially the spinach. Season with salt and pepper. Serve at once, or if time allows, let the soup stand off the heat for an hour or two.

5 The soup thickens as it stands. Adjust the consistency with more water as needed; taste and adjust the seasonings. Reheat before serving.

KALE, SQUASH & SWEET POTATO STEW

A sturdy medley of colorful seasonal vegetables   6 to 8 servings

In this hearty, early autumn harvest stew, the deep green color of the kale contrasts beautifully with the vivid yellow and orange hues of summer squash and sweet potatoes, making it pleasing to both the eyes and the palate.

1 tablespoon olive oil
1 medium-large red onion, chopped
2 to 3 cloves garlic, minced
6 to 8 ounces kale (any variety)
2 to 3 medium sweet potatoes,
    peeled and diced
32-ounce carton vegetable broth or 4 cups
    water with 2 vegetable bouillon cubes
1 teaspoon grated fresh or bottled ginger
1 teaspoon dry mustard
1 to 2 teaspoons sweet or smoked paprika
2 small yellow summer squashes, diced
2 medium-large ripe tomatoes, diced
2 tablespoons balsamic vinegar, or to taste
Salt and freshly ground pepper to taste
Hot cooked quinoa, brown rice, barley,
    or farro for serving, optional

1   Heat the oil in a soup pot. Add the onion and sauté over medium-low heat until translucent. Add the garlic and continue to sauté until both are golden.

2   Trim away and discard the thick midribs from the kale leaves. Chop the kale into bite-sized pieces and rinse well in a colander. Add to the soup pot along with the sweet potatoes and broth. Stir in the ginger, mustard, and paprika. Bring to a slow boil, then lower the heat. Simmer gently over low heat with the cover ajar for about 10 minutes.

3   Stir in the squash and tomatoes, and simmer until the kale and sweet potato dice are tender, about 15 to 20 minutes. Mash enough of the sweet potato dice with the back of a wooden spoon to thicken the base.

4   Season with balsamic vinegar, salt, and pepper. If time allows, let the stew stand off the heat for an hour or two.

5   Adjust the consistency with a little more water, if need be, and taste for salt and pepper. Reheat before serving. If you'd like, serve over hot cooked grain of your choice to make this stew even more substantial.

ROASTED BUTTERNUT MISO SOUP

With soba noodles and spinach 6 servings

Once you've baked the squash, this simple and pretty Japanese-inspired soup comes together quickly. Save a bit of time and effort by using pre-diced butternut squash, which is easy to find in the produce section of well-stocked supermarkets throughout fall and winter.

20-ounce package fresh diced
   butternut squash
Olive oil
32-ounce carton vegetable broth or 4 cups
   water with 2 vegetable bouillon cubes
4 ounces soba (buckwheat
   noodles), broken in half
1 teaspoon grated fresh or bottled
   ginger, or more, to taste
5 ounces baby spinach
1 cup frozen green peas, thawed
2 rounded tablespoons miso,
   or more, to taste
Freshly ground pepper to taste
2 scallions, green parts only, thinly sliced
Fresh cilantro leaves, optional

1 Preheat the oven to 400° F. Arrange the diced squash in a parchment-lined roasting pan. Drizzle with a little olive oil and bake for 25 to 30 minutes, or until tender and touched with golden brown spots here and there. Stir every few minutes while in the oven. This step can be done ahead of time.

2 Bring the broth to a simmer in a soup pot. Add the soba and ginger and cook until the noodles are *al dente*.

3 Add the spinach, peas, and roasted squash. Cook just until the spinach is wilted, but still bright green, and everything is well heated through. If the ingredients are crowded, add 1 cup of water at a time, until the soup has the consistency you like.

4 Dissolve the miso in about ⅓ cup warm water and stir into the soup. Taste, and if you'd like to add more, repeat the process with 1 tablespoon of miso at a time.

5 Season with pepper and serve at once. Garnish each serving with a little scallion and optional cilantro.

SPAGHETTI SQUASH STEW

With a crisp vegetable topping

6 to 8 servings

If it's possible for a vegetable to be considered a "fun" food, it would be spaghetti squash. Its noodle-like strands contrast nicely with the crisp topping of turnips and snow peas.

1 medium spaghetti squash

2 tablespoons olive oil

1 large onion, quartered and thinly sliced

2 cloves garlic, minced

28-ounce can fire roasted diced tomatoes

⅓ cup thinly sliced sun-dried
   tomatoes, oil cured or not

2 cups water

1 cup small white or cremini mushrooms,
   stemmed and thinly sliced

2 teaspoons salt-free seasoning
   (see page 8 for brands)

½ teaspoon dried oregano

¼ teaspoon dried thyme

Salt and freshly ground pepper to taste

1 pound turnips or jícama, peeled
   and cut into thick matchsticks

1 heaping cup snow peas or
   snap peas, trimmed

1 Preheat the oven to 375° F.

2 Cut the squash in half lengthwise, then scrape out the seeds. Place the two halves, cut side up, in a foil-lined shallow casserole dish. Cover tightly with more foil and bake for 40 to 50 minutes, or until easily pierced with a fork.

3 When the squash is cool enough to handle, scrape the flesh away from the shell with a fork, using downward motions to remove the spaghetti-like strands.

4 Heat 1 tablespoon of the oil in a soup pot. Add the onion and sauté over medium-low heat until translucent. Add the garlic and continue to sauté until the onion is just beginning to brown.

5 Add the spaghetti squash, fire roasted and sun-dried tomatoes, water, mushrooms, seasoning, oregano, and thyme. Bring to a slow boil, then lower the heat. Simmer gently over low heat with the cover ajar for 20 to 25 minutes. Adjust the consistency with more water if need be; season with salt and pepper.

6 Meanwhile, heat the remaining tablespoon of oil in a skillet or stir-fry pan. Add the turnips and sauté over medium-high heat, stirring frequently, until golden. Add the snow peas and continue to sauté, stirring, until the snow peas are bright green and tender-crisp.

7 Serve at once. Top each serving with some of the turnips and snow peas.

ORANGE BUTTERNUT SQUASH SOUP

With sautéed jícama and red onion   6 servings

With its cheerful hue, this soup has a hint of sweetness and the pleasant crunch of jícama. Once you've got the squash baked, the rest is a snap.

1 medium butternut squash,
    about 1 ½ pounds
2 tablespoons olive oil or fragrant
    nut oil (such as walnut)
1 large red onion, quartered
    and thinly sliced
3 cups water
1 cup orange juice, preferably
    freshly squeezed
2 cups frozen green peas
3 to 4 scallions, thinly sliced
2 teaspoons good-quality curry powder
1 teaspoon grated fresh or bottled ginger
¼ teaspoon cinnamon
Pinch of nutmeg
1 medium jícama, peeled and
    cut into ½-inch dice
Salt and freshly ground pepper to taste

1 Preheat the oven to 375° F. Halve the squash lengthwise and place, cut side up, in a foil-lined shallow baking dish. Cover with more foil. Bake for 45 to 50 minutes, or until easily pierced through with a knife. (If you don't have a knife sharp enough to cut the squash, simply wrap the whole thing in foil, place in the baking dish and bake until done.) When the squash is cool enough to handle, scoop out and discard the seeds and fibers. Scoop the flesh from the peel and transfer to a food processor.

2 Heat 1 tablespoon of the oil in a soup pot. Add the onion and sauté over medium-low heat until golden, stirring frequently. Remove half of the onion and set aside. Transfer the rest to the food processor and process with the squash until smoothly pureed.

3 Transfer the puree to the soup pot. Add the water and the orange juice and stir together. Add the peas, scallions, curry, ginger, cinnamon, and nutmeg. Bring to a slow boil, then lower the heat. Simmer gently over low heat with the cover ajar for 10 minutes.

4 Heat the remaining oil in a medium skillet. Add the jícama and sauté over medium-high heat until touched with golden spots, stirring frequently.

5 Season with salt and pepper. If need be, adjust the consistency with more water or orange juice, then adjust the seasonings. Stir the jícama and reserved onion into the soup, or use them to top each bowlful. If time allows, let the soup stand off the heat for an hour or so, then reheat before serving.

PUMPKIN APPLE SOUP

With sweet spices and toasted nuts

Make this soup a few hours ahead of time, if you can. The offbeat combination of flavors benefits from having time to blend. Use butternut squash instead of pumpkin, if you prefer.

1 sugar pumpkin, about 2 pounds
1 ½ tablespoons olive oil
1 large onion, finely chopped
2 medium celery stalks, finely diced
2 medium tart apples, peeled,
    cored, and diced
32-ounce carton vegetable broth or 4 cups
    water with 2 vegetable bouillon cubes
2 teaspoons grated fresh or bottled ginger
1 teaspoon good-quality curry powder
½ teaspoon cinnamon
¼ teaspoon nutmeg
2 cups unsweetened plant-based
    milk, or more, as needed
Salt and freshly ground pepper to taste
½ cup chopped toasted almonds
    or cashews for garnish
Chopped fresh parsley for garnish

1 Preheat the oven to 375° F. Halve the pumpkin lengthwise and place, cut side up, in a foil-lined shallow baking dish. Cover with more foil. Bake for 45 to 50 minutes, or until it can be easily pierced with a knife. This step can be done ahead of time. When cool enough to handle, scoop out and discard the seeds and fibers. Peel the pumkin and cut the flesh into large dice.

2 Heat the oil in a soup pot. Add the onion and celery and sauté over medium-low heat until both are golden.

3 Add the pumpkin, apples, broth, ginger, and spices. Bring to a slow boil, then lower the heat. Simmer gently over low heat with the cover ajar for 20 to 25 minutes, or until the pumpkin and apple are tender.

4 Transfer the solid ingredients to a food processor and puree completely or leave a bit chunky. You can also puree just half of the solid ingredients for more texture, if you prefer. Transfer the puree back to the soup pot. Or, skip the food processor and insert an immersion blender into the pot and blend the soup until pureed to your liking.

5 Stir in enough plant-based milk to give the soup a slightly thick consistency. Season with salt and pepper and remove from the heat.

6 Serve at once, or allow the soup to stand off the heat for an hour or two. Taste to adjust the seasonings, then reheat before serving. Garnish each bowlful with a sprinkling of chopped nuts and parsley.

MOROCCAN-STYLE VEGETABLE STEW

With winter squash, chickpeas, and couscous   6 or more servings

This delicious stew looks and smells as enticing as it tastes — it's a feast of fall flavors in a simple, aromatic broth.

1 small sugar pumpkin or medium
    butternut squash, about 1 ½ pounds
1 ½ tablespoons olive oil
2 large onions, chopped
2 medium potatoes, scrubbed
    and cut into ¾-inch chunks
2 large or 3 to 4 medium carrots,
    peeled and coarsely chopped
14.5-ounce can diced tomatoes
    (try fire roasted)
2 teaspoons ground cumin
½ teaspoon turmeric
15-ounce can chickpeas, drained and rinsed
Salt and freshly ground pepper to taste
2 cups water
1 cup raw couscous
¼ to ½ cup chopped fresh parsley, to taste

1 Preheat the oven to 375° F. Halve the pumpkin lengthwise and place, cut side up, in a foil-lined shallow baking dish. Cover with more foil. Bake for 40 to 45 minutes, or until it can be pierced with a knife, with some resistance. This step can be done ahead of time. When cool enough to handle, scoop out and discard the seeds and fibers. Peel and cut into large dice.

2 Heat the oil in a soup pot. Add the onions and sauté over medium-low heat until golden.

3 Add the potatoes, pumpkin, carrots, tomatoes, cumin, and turmeric. Add enough water to cover all but about ½ inch of the vegetables. Bring to a slow boil, then lower the heat. Simmer gently over low heat with the cover ajar for 35 to 40 minutes, or until the vegetables are tender.

4 Stir in the chickpeas, then season with salt and pepper. Simmer over very low heat for 10 to 15 minutes longer.

5 Meanwhile, bring the water to a boil in a small saucepan. Stir in the couscous, cover, and remove from the heat. Let stand for 10 minutes or so, then fluff with a fork.

6 To serve the stew, place a small amount of the couscous in each soup bowl, then ladle some stew over it and sprinkle with parsley. Serve at once.

MOROCCAN LENTIL & CHICKPEA SOUP

Two flavorful legumes in a gently spiced broth

Called Harira *in Arabic, this classic soup features the compatible duo of lentils and chickpeas. It can be served year-round but is especially appealing as a transitional early fall soup using fresh tomatoes. It's delicious served with fresh pita or other flatbread.*

2 tablespoons olive oil
1 large onion, finely chopped
3 large celery stalks, diced
2 cloves garlic, minced
¾ cup dried brown or green lentils, rinsed
1 teaspoon turmeric
1 teaspoon cumin
1 to 2 teaspoons grated fresh or
 bottled ginger, to taste
½ teaspoon cinnamon
5 cups water
2 cups diced ripe tomatoes, or a
 14.5-ounce can diced tomatoes
15-ounce can chickpeas, drained and rinsed
Juice of ½ lemon (slice the rest
 thinly for garnish)
¼ cup chopped fresh parsley,
 or more to taste
Salt and freshly ground pepper to taste

1 Heat the oil in a soup pot. Add the onions and sauté over medium-low heat until translucent, about 5 minutes. Add the celery and garlic and sauté until all are golden, about 5 to 7 minutes.

2 Add the lentils, spices, and water. Bring to a slow boil, then lower the heat. Simmer gently over low heat with the cover ajar until the lentils are just tender, about 30 minutes.

3 Stir in the tomatoes and chickpeas. Adjust the consistency with more water if needed (but let it remain thick), and adjust the spices to taste. Simmer for 10 to 15 minutes longer over low heat.

4 Stir in the lemon juice and parsley, then season with salt and pepper. Garnishing each serving with thin lemon slices.

CHICKPEA & TAHINI SOUP

With mushrooms and lots of fresh herbs

The classic Middle Eastern team of chickpeas and tahini (sesame paste) is highlighted in a tasty, offbeat soup. Serve with fresh pita bread and tabbouli salad for a lovely meal.

1 tablespoon olive oil

1 medium onion, chopped

3 to 4 cloves garlic, minced

32-ounce carton vegetable broth or 4 cups
    water with 2 vegetable bouillon cubes

2 cups sliced white or cremini mushrooms

1 cup finely shredded white cabbage

1 teaspoon ground cumin

2 teaspoons salt-free seasoning
    (see page 8 for brands)

3 to 3 ½ cups cooked chickpeas, or two
    15-ounce cans, drained and rinsed

¼ cup tahini

¼ to ½ cup finely chopped
    fresh parsley, to taste

3 to 4 scallions, thinly sliced

2 to 3 tablespoons minced fresh
    dill, or more, to taste

Juice of ½ to 1 lemon, to taste

Salt and freshly ground pepper to taste

1   Heat the oil in a soup pot. Add the onion and sauté over medium-low heat until translucent. Add the garlic and continue to sauté until both are golden.

2   Add the broth, mushrooms, cabbage, and seasonings. Bring to a slow boil, then lower the heat. Simmer gently over low heat with the cover ajar for 15 minutes.

3   Meanwhile, set aside 1 cup of the chickpeas and place the remainder in a food processor or blender with the tahini. Add a little water as needed to thin the consistency. Process until smoothly pureed. Stir the puree back into the soup pot.

4   Stir in the reserved chickpeas and simmer gently for 10 minutes.

5   Stir in the parsley, scallions, dill, and lemon juice. Add water as needed for a medium-thick consistency.

6   Season with salt and pepper, then simmer gently for 3 to 4 minutes longer. Serve at once.

SOUTHWESTERN FRESH CORN STEW

With green beans and chili peppers   6 servings

When fresh local corn is abundant in the late summer and early fall, the most tempting way to eat it is right off the cob. But cooking with fresh corn can be equally appealing. Its sweetness can't be matched by frozen corn kernels.

1 tablespoon olive oil

1 large onion, chopped

2 to 3 cloves garlic, minced

4 medium ears fresh corn

2 medium-large ripe tomatoes, diced

14.5-ounce can pureed or crushed tomatoes

2 small yellow summer squashes,
    cut into ¾-inch diced

1 ½ to 2 cups fresh slender green
    beans, trimmed and cut into
    1-inch lengths (see Note)

1 to 2 fresh mild chilis (such as Anaheim
    or poblano), seeded and minced

3 cups water, or as needed

Salt and freshly ground pepper to taste

¼ to ½ cup finely chopped
    fresh cilantro, to taste

Vegan sour cream (homemade, page 7,
    or from an 8-ounce tub), optional

1   Heat the oil in a soup pot. Add the onion and sauté over medium-low heat until translucent. Add the garlic and continue to sauté until both are golden.

2   Break each ear of corn in half. Stand each on its flat end and scrape the kernels from the cobs with a sharp knife. Place them in a bowl as you go along.

3   Add the corn kernels to the soup pot along with the fresh and canned tomatoes, diced squash, green beans, and chilis.

4   Add the water, more or less as needed for a stew-like consistency. Bring to a slow boil, then lower the heat. Simmer gently over low heat with the cover ajar for 20 minutes, or until the vegetables are tender.

5   Season with salt and pepper, then stir in the cilantro. Serve at once. Top each serving with sour cream, if desired.

NOTE If you can't find green beans that are fresh and tender, use frozen green beans. Thaw the green beans completely before using them.

VARIATION Add a cup or two of cooked pinto or pink beans to the stew to make it even heartier.

AUTUMN HARVEST STEW

A lively medley of early fall produce

This colorful stew of sweet potatoes and greens, embellished with fresh corn and tomatoes, is a perfect way to showcase late summer/early fall produce.

2 tablespoons olive oil

1 large yellow or red onion, chopped

2 cloves garlic, minced

2 large or 3 medium sweet
  potatoes, peeled and diced

32-ounce carton vegetable broth or 4 cups
  water with 2 vegetable bouillon cubes

10 to 12 ounces hardy greens (collard
  greens, kale, or chard)

2 cups fresh corn kernels
  (from 3 medium ears)

1 medium yellow summer squash, diced

2 cups diced ripe tomatoes

2 teaspoons salt-free seasoning
  (see page 8 for brands)

1 teaspoon ground cumin, or more, to taste

Fresh cilantro or parsley, as desired

Dried hot red pepper flakes
  or sriracha, to taste

Salt and freshly ground pepper to taste

1 Heat the oil in a soup pot. Add the onion and sauté over medium-low heat until translucent. Add the garlic and continue to sauté until both are golden.

2 Add the sweet potatoes and broth. Bring to a slow boil, then lower the heat. Simmer over low heat with the cover ajar for 10 to 15 minutes.

3 Meanwhile, cut the greens away from the stems. Stack several leaves at a time, roll up snugly from the narrow end closest to you, then cut them into thin strips. Chop the strips in a few places to shorten them. Give them a good rinse in a colander. Chard stems may be thinly sliced and used; discard kale and collard stems.

4 Once the sweet potatoes are nearly tender, stir in the greens, corn, squash, tomatoes, and cumin. Continue to simmer until the greens and corn are just tender, about 10 minutes. Mash some of the sweet potato dice with the back of a wooden spoon to thicken the base.

5 Stir in the cilantro and add just enough hot seasoning to give the stew a subtle heat. Season with salt and pepper. Serve at once, or, if time allows, let the stew stand off the heat for an hour or two. Heat through before serving.

CASHEW BRUSSELS SPROUTS SOUP

With hints of wine and lemon

The secret ingredient that makes this soup so rich and luscious is raw cashews. Fresh whole grain bread and a simple salad make excellent companions.

1 tablespoon olive oil
1 large onion, chopped
1 large celery stalk, chopped
1 clove garlic, minced
1 large potato, peeled and diced
1 large tomato, diced
1 ½ pounds Brussels sprouts,
   trimmed and coarsely chopped
1 ½ cups (about 6 ounces) raw cashews
6 cups water
2 vegetable bouillon cubes
2 teaspoons salt-free seasoning
   (see page 8 for brands)
¼ cup dry white wine, optional
2 tablespoons lemon juice, or to taste
Salt and freshly ground pepper to
   taste (lemon pepper is great!)
Chopped fresh parsley for garnish
Chopped toasted cashews
   for garnish, optional

1 Heat the oil in a soup pot. Add the onion, celery, and garlic and sauté over medium-low heat until all are golden.

2 Add the potato, tomato, about two-thirds of the Brussels sprouts (reserve and set aside the remainder), cashews, water, bouillon cubes, seasoning, and optional wine.

3 Bring to a slow boil, then lower the heat. Simmer gently over low heat with the cover ajar for 20 to 25 minutes, or until all the vegetables are tender. Remove from the heat.

4 Transfer the solid ingredients to a food processor or blender with a little of the liquid and puree in batches until smooth. Transfer back to the soup pot. Or, skip the food processor and insert an immersion blender into the pot and blend the soup until pureed to your liking.

5 In a separate saucepan, steam the reserved Brussels sprouts in about an inch of water until bright green and tender-crisp. Stir them into the soup.

6 Adjust the consistency with a little more water if needed. Add the lemon juice, salt, and pepper. Heat through and serve.

7 Garnish each serving with a little parsley and a sprinkling of toasted cashews, if desired.

CHARD STEW WITH TORTELLINI

An aromatic bowlful highlighting the abundant leafy green   8 or more servings

---

Here's a bountiful stew made with chard, a beloved vegetable in Italian cuisine, and the delightful addition of vegan tortellini.

⅔ cup sun-dried tomatoes (not oil-cured), cut into strips

1 large bunch green or rainbow chard (at least 10 ounces)

1 tablespoon extra-virgin olive oil

1 medium onion, finely chopped

2 cloves garlic, minced

2 medium carrots, peeled and thinly sliced

4 cups water

14.5-ounce can diced tomatoes (Italian-style or fire roasted)

10- to 12-ounce package frozen vegan tortellini (tofu or vegetable-filled), partially thawed

2 teaspooons salt-free seasoning (see page 8 for brands)

1 ½ teaspoons Italian seasoning

1 medium yellow summer squash, diced

Salt and freshly ground pepper to taste

Sliced basil leaves, as desired

1   Cover the dried tomatoes with about a cup of boiling water in a small bowl. Let stand until needed.

2   Cut the chard leaves away from the thick midribs. Chop the leaves into bite-size pieces and slice the midribs thinly. Rinse them all well in a colander. Set aside until needed.

3   Heat the oil in a large soup pot. Add the onion, garlic, and carrots and sauté over medium-low heat until all are golden.

4   Add the water, tomatoes, tortellini, and seasonings to the soup pot. Bring to a slow boil, then lower the heat. Simmer gently over low heat with the cover ajar for 15 minutes, or until the carrots are just tender.

5   Add the squash. Continue to simmer over low heat for 5 to 6 minutes longer, or until the tortellini and the squash are nearly done.

6   Stir the chard into the soup pot. Add more water, if needed, to give the stew a moist, not too soupy consistency. Continue to cook until the chard is just tender, about 5 minutes.

7   Season with salt and pepper, then serve at once. Garnish each serving with basil leaves.

BROCCOLI PEANUT SOUP

Subtly mellowed with apple   6 servings

Luscious and nutty, with a touch of sweetness, peanut butter gives this soup a rich flavor. In my home, this is a longtime fall favorite!

1 ½ tablespoons olive oil
2 large onions, chopped
2 cloves garlic, minced
3 medium carrots, peeled and sliced
32-ounce carton vegetable broth or 4 cups
    water with 2 vegetable bouillon cubes
2 medium apples, peeled, cored, and diced
1 teaspoon good quality curry powder
⅔ cup creamy peanut butter
6 heaping cups finely chopped
    broccoli (mainly florets; some
    tender stems are fine)
Juice of ½ lemon
Salt and freshly ground pepper to taste
Pinch of dried hot red pepper flakes,
    plus more to pass around
Chopped roasted peanuts
    for garnish, optional

1   Heat the oil in a soup pot. Add the onions and sauté over medium-low heat until translucent. Add the garlic and carrots and continue to sauté until all are golden.

2   Add the broth along with the apples and curry powder. Bring to a slow boil, then lower the heat. Simmer gently over low heat with the cover ajar for 10 to 15 minutes, or until the carrots and apple are tender. Remove from the heat.

3   Transfer the solid ingredients from the soup pot to a food processor with a slotted spoon. Process until just coarsely pureed, leaving some chunkiness. Stir back into the soup pot. Or, skip the food processor and insert an immersion blender into the pot and process until coarsely pureed.

4   Add the peanut butter to the soup, about half at a time, whisking it in until completely blended. Return to very low heat.

5   Steam the broccoli in a saucepan with about ¼ cup water, covered, for 5 minutes, or until brightly green and tender-crisp to your liking. Stir into the soup.

6   If the soup is too thick, add enough water to give it a medium-thick consistency. Stir in the lemon juice, then season with salt, pepper, and red pepper flakes.

7   Serve at once. Pass around more red pepper flakes and chopped peanuts for topping individual servings, if desired.

SWEET & SAUERKRAUT SOUP

Topped with vegan sausage   6 to 8 servings

This hearty soup is a great choice for nippy fall evenings, delicious served with fresh sourdough or rye bread. Make sure to look for naturally fermented sauerkraut, which contains valuable probiotics. The kind that comes in cans is briny, but not fermented.

3 tablespoons olive oil

1 large onion, quartered and thinly sliced

2 medium carrots, peeled and thinly sliced

1 large celery stalk, finely diced

32-ounce carton vegetable broth or 4 cups
   water with 2 vegetable bouillon cubes

3 medium golden potatoes, peeled
   (or scrubbed) and diced

2 medium apples, peeled and diced

2 cups naturally fermented
   sauerkraut (from a jar), drained

14.5-ounce can diced tomatoes

2 teaspoons salt-free seasoning
   (see page 8 for brands)

15-ounce can small white beans,
   drained and rinsed

2 tablespoons natural granulated
   sugar, more or less to taste

Salt and freshly ground pepper to taste

14-ounce package vegan
   sausage links, sliced

1   Heat half of the oil in a soup pot. Add the onion, carrots, and celery, and sauté over medium-low heat until all are golden.

2   Add the broth and potatoes. Bring to a slow boil, then lower the heat. Simmer gently over low heat with the cover ajar for 15 minutes, or until the potatoes are just tender.

3   Stir in the apples, sauerkraut, tomatoes, seasoning, and beans. Simmer for 15 to 20 minutes longer, or until everything is tender.

4   Adjust the consistency with a bit more water if the soup is crowded. Add sugar in small amounts to balance the tartness of the sauerkraut, tasting as you add. Season with salt and pepper (you may need very little salt, if any). If time allows, let the soup stand off the heat for an hour or so.

5   Heat the remaining oil in a medium skillet. Add the sliced sausage and sauté over medium-high heat, stirring frequently, until touched with golden brown here and there.

6   Reheat the soup as needed before serving and top each bowlful with some of the sausage slices.

VARIATION If you're a kimchi fan, swap it in for the sauerkraut.

GARLICKY CREAM OF CELERY SOUP

A perfect puree for a chilly fall day   6 servings

This smooth soup will win you over with its elegant simplicity and intense celery flavor. There are no better companion than Garlic Croutons (page 25).

12 large celery stalks
2 tablespoons olive oil
1 large onion, chopped
8 cloves garlic, minced
2 tablespoons unbleached white flour
3 medium potatoes, peeled and diced
2 teaspoons salt-free seasoning
   (see page 8 for brands)
½ cup fresh parsley leaves
2 to 4 tablespoons chopped
   fresh dill, to taste
Handful of celery leaves, chopped
1 ½ cups unsweetened plant-based
   milk, or more, as needed
Salt and freshly ground pepper to taste
Chopped fresh parsley and/or
   dill for garnish

1 Trim the bottoms from the celery stalks and remove the strings with a vegetable peeler. Cut 10 of the stalks into ½-inch slices. Cut the remaining two into ¼-inch dice, and set aside.

2 Heat one tablespoon of the oil in a soup pot. Add the onion and garlic and sauté over medium-low heat until both are golden.

3 Sprinkle in the flour and stir in until it disappears. Add the celery, potatoes, and seasoning along with just enough water to cover the vegetables. Bring to a slow boil, then lower the heat. Simmer gently over low heat with the cover ajar until the vegetables are tender, about 25 minutes.

4 Add the parsley, dill, and celery leaves.

5 With a slotted spoon, transfer the solid ingredients to a food processor or blender with a little of the liquid. Process (in batches if necessary), until smoothly pureed, then stir back into the soup pot. Or, skip the food processor and insert an immersion blender into the pot and blend the soup until pureed to your liking.

6 Return to low heat and add enough plant-based milk to give the soup a slightly thick consistency.

7 Heat the remaining oil in a small skillet. Add the reserved celery and sauté over medium heat until touched with golden spots. Stir into the soup, then season with salt and pepper.

8 Serve at once, or allow the soup to stand off the heat for an hour or so, then heat through before serving. Garnish each serving with chopped herbs.

CARROT GINGER SOUP

A beautiful orange bowlful with a parsnip variation

6 to 8 servings

This pureed carrot soup is a concentrated and colorful bowl of nourishment. Let's face it, though—peeling and chopping two pounds of carrots is a bit of a project. A quicker route to this brilliant-hued soup is to use two bags of baby carrots. Try the variation, which calls for replacing half of the carrots with parsnips, another economical cool-weather vegetable.

1 tablespoon olive oil
1 large onion, chopped
2 to 3 cloves garlic, minced
Two 16-ounce bags baby carrots
   (see parsnip variation)
14.5-ounce can diced tomatoes (try fire
   roasted or Italian-style for extra flavor)
2 to 3 teaspoons grated fresh
   or bottled ginger
1 ½ to 2 cups unsweetened plant-based
   milk, or more, as needed
Juice and zest of 1 orange
Salt and freshly ground pepper to taste
Chopped parsley or cilantro for garnish

1 Heat the oil in a soup pot. Add the onion and sauté over medium-low heat until translucent. Add the garlic and continue to sauté until both are golden.

2 Add the carrots, tomatoes, and ginger along with enough water to barely cover the vegetables.

3 Bring to a slow boil, then lower the heat. Simmer gently over low heat with the cover ajar until the carrots are tender. This will take from 20 to 30 minutes, depending on their thickness. Remove from the heat.

4 Transfer the cooked vegetables, along with a little of the cooking liquid, to a blender or food processor. Process in batches to a smooth consistency and return the puree to the soup pot. Or, skip the blender and insert an immersion blender into the pot and blend the soup until pureed to your liking.

5 Stir in enough plant-based milk to give the soup a medium-thick consistency. Return to low heat. Add the orange juice and zest, then season to taste with salt and pepper. Garnish with parsley and serve.

VARIATION Use one 16-ounce bag baby carrots plus 16 ounces fresh parsnips (if not sold loose, they also often come in 16-ounce bags). It's debatable whether parsnips need to be peeled. If they're small and look fresh, you can simply scrub them well — especially if you'll be using a blender rather than an immersion blender. If the parsnips are large, it's best to peel them.

KIMCHI SOUP

A bold Korean classic made plant-based

6 to 8 servings

Kimchi soup (Jjigae) is a Korean classic that's easy to adapt to a plant-based version. Don't be daunted by the ingredient list — this is super-easy to make and ready to eat quickly. Brimming with Korean seasonings and briny kimchi, the broth becomes flavorful in no time.

14-ounce tub extra-firm tofu

1 tablespoon toasted sesame oil
  or neutral vegetable oil

1 medium onion, finely chopped

3 to 4 cloves garlic, minced

4 cups napa cabbage, sliced

6 to 8 ounces mushrooms, any variety,
  cleaned, stemmed, and sliced

2 teaspoons grated fresh or bottled
  ginger, or more, to taste

1 teaspoon gochugaru, or more, to taste

6 cups water, plus more, as needed

2 vegetable bouillon cubes

2 tablespoons soy sauce

14.5-ounce can diced tomatoes
  (fire-roasted, if available)

4 stalks bok choy or 1 medium
  baby bok choy, sliced

1 tablespoon gochujang paste,
  more or less to taste

1 cup vegan kimchi, mild or
  medium, or more, if desired

2 scallions, thinly sliced plus more
  (green parts) for topping

⅓ cup fresh cilantro leaves,
  plus more for topping

1   Cut the tofu into 6 slabs crosswise and blot well between layers of clean tea towels or paper towels (or, if you have a tofu press, use it ahead of time). Cut the slabs into dice and set aside.

2   Heat the oil in a soup pot. Add the onion and sauté over medium-low heat until translucent. Add the garlic and continue to sauté until both are golden.

3   Add the cabbage, mushrooms, ginger, gochugaru, water, bouillon cubes, soy sauce, and tomatoes. Bring to a slow boil, then turn down the heat. Simmer gently over low heat with the cover ajar until the cabbage and mushrooms are wilted, about 5 minutes.

4   Add the reserved tofu, bok choy, gochujang paste, kimchi, and scallions. The broth will likely be a bit crowded, so add 1 to 2 cups of water, or more as needed. Continue to cook over low heat for 5 minutes, or just until everything is piping hot.

5   Remove from the heat. Season with salt and stir in the cilantro. Serve at once. Top each serving with a little extra scallion and cilantro.

HOT & SOUR VEGETABLE SOUP

An extravaganza of invigorating textures and flavors   6 servings

Hot and sour soup is surprisingly easy to make, doesn't take long to cook, and is full of robust textures and flavors. The trick is to adjust the spicy, salty, and sour flavors to your liking.

1 tablespoon neutral vegetable oil
2 teaspoons dark sesame oil
1 medium-large onion, quartered
    and thinly sliced
2 to 3 cloves garlic, minced
14.5-ounce can fire roasted diced tomatoes
1 cup fresh shiitake mushrooms,
    stemmed and sliced
5 cups water
3 to 4 stalks bok choy, stems sliced,
    leaves chopped, and well rinsed
1 cup snow peas, trimmed and
    cut into 1-inch pieces
15-ounce can baby corn with liquid
3 to 4 tablespoons rice vinegar, to taste
Chili oil, sriracha, or other hot
    seasoning, to taste
2 tablespoons soy sauce, or to taste
¼ teaspoon black pepper, or to taste
1 to 2 tablespoons natural granulated sugar
8 ounces extra-firm tofu, well drained
    and cut into ½-inch dice
2 to 3 scallions, thinly sliced
2 tablespoons cornstarch or arrowroot

1   Heat both oils in a soup pot. Add the onion and sauté over medium-low heat until translucent. Add the garlic and continue to sauté until both are golden.

2   Add the tomatoes, shiitakes, and water. Bring to a slow boil, then lower the heat. Simmer gently over low heat with the cover ajar for 5 minutes.

3   Add the remaining ingredients except the cornstarch. Taste frequently as you add the vinegar, hot seasoning, soy sauce, pepper, and sugar.

4   Dissolve the cornstarch in ¼ cup water. Slowly drizzle into the soup while stirring.

5   Simmer over low heat for 2 minutes. If the soup is too crowded, add another cup or so of water. Serve at once.

BUDDHA'S DELIGHT STEW

Featuring seitan, green vegetables, and mushrooms   6 to 8 servings

Inspired by a favorite vegetarian Chinese restaurant dish, this stew is enhanced with protein-packed seitan (cooked wheat gluten). Though seitan is widely available in natural foods stores, consider making your own! My seitan recipe is one of the most popular on the web — do a search for "easy homemade seitan recipe" at TheVeganAtlas.com. If you're on a gluten-free diet, consider swapping in tofu for the seitan and using GF soy sauce.

1 large broccoli crown, cut
   into bite-size pieces
2 cups fresh green beans, trimmed
   and cut into 1-inch pieces
3 large carrots, peeled and sliced diagonally
2 cloves garlic, minced
32-ounce carton vegetable broth, or
   Dried Shiitake Mushroom Broth
   (page 14; include the mushrooms)
12 to 16 ounces packaged or
   homemade seitan (see headnote),
   cut into bite-size chunks
1 ½ cups small cremini or white mushrooms,
   cleaned, stemmed, and sliced
15-ounce can baby corn, with liquid
4 to 6 ounces fine rice noodles
   (Asian rice vermicelli)
3 tablespoons cornstarch
3 tablespoons soy sauce or
   tamari, or to taste
Freshly ground pepper and/or dried
   hot red pepper flakes to taste

1 Combine the broccoli, green beans, carrots, garlic, and broth in a soup pot. Bring to a slow boil, then lower the heat. Simmer gently over low heat with the cover ajar for 5 minutes, or until the broccoli and green beans turn bright green.

2 Add the seitan, mushrooms, and baby corn (with liquid). Cook over medium-high heat, uncovered, until all the vegetables are tender-crisp, about 8 minutes.

3 Meanwhile, in a separate saucepan, cook the noodles according to package directions until *al dente*, then drain and cut into shorter lengths. Set aside until needed.

4 Put the cornstarch in a small bowl or mixing cup and stir in just enough of the broth from the soup pot to smoothly dissolve it. Slowly pour into the soup pot and simmer just until the broth has thickened.

5 Stir in the cooked rice noodles. Season with soy sauce and pepper, and serve at once.

QUINOA PEANUT VEGETABLE SOUP

A feast of chunky vegetables in a nutty base   6 to 8 servings

---

This easy, robust soup, contributed by longtime reader Marty Hall, has several elements of a certain style of traditional African soups—chilis, sweet potato, and a creamy peanut base. The grain of choice in an African soup would most likely be millet, but here, quinoa, the nutritious South American supergrain, heightens the nutty flavor and cooks more quickly.

2 tablespoons olive oil
1 large red onion, chopped
2 to 4 cloves garlic, minced
1 medium red bell pepper, diced
2 celery stalks, diced
1 to 2 fresh jalapeño peppers,
    seeded and minced
Handful of celery leaves, chopped
1 large sweet potato, peeled and diced
6 cups water
2 vegetable bouillon cubes
1 medium zucchini, quartered
    lengthwise and sliced
1 teaspoon ground cumin
1 teaspoon dried oregano
1 teaspoon grated fresh or bottled ginger
½ cup raw quinoa
½ cup smooth natural peanut butter
Salt and freshly ground pepper to taste
Cayenne pepper, or dried hot
    red pepper flakes, to taste

1   Heat the oil in a soup pot. Sauté the onion over medium-low heat until translucent, then add the garlic, bell pepper, and celery. Continue to sauté until all are golden.

2   Add the remaining ingredients except the last three. Bring to a slow boil, then lower the heat. Simmer gently over low heat with the cover ajar until quinoa is cooked and vegetables are tender, about 15 minutes.

3   Add the peanut butter, stirring well to blend in completely, then simmer over low heat for 10 minutes longer, or until the quinoa is puffy and the sweet potato is tender.

4   Season with salt, pepper, and cayenne. If time allows, let the soup stand off the heat for an hour or so. It will thicken as it stands.

5   Just before serving, adjust the consistency with water as needed. Adjust the seasonings, then reheat and serve.

WINTER

Winter is the very best time for hearty soups and stews—nothing offers better comfort to body and spirit when coming in from the cold. What a perfect time to make thick soups of grains and legumes. Teamed with bread and salad, most of the soups in this section make satisfying meals in and of themselves.

MINESTRONE

An easy take on classic Italian vegetable soup   8 or more servings

Filling and flavorful, this classic soup becomes a meal in itself when served with a robust bread like Focaccia (page 22) or a whole grain Italian loaf. This soup keeps well and develops flavor as it stands.

2 tablespoons extra-virgin olive oil
2 medium onions, finely chopped
2 to 3 cloves garlic, minced
2 medium carrots, peeled and diced
2 medium celery stalks, diced
Handful of celery leaves
2 medium potatoes, peeled and diced
14.5-ounce can Italian-style diced tomatoes
14.5-ounce can tomato sauce
   or crushed tomatoes
¼ cup dry red wine, optional
2 teaspoons Italian seasoning
15-ounce can chickpeas, drained and rinsed
1 cup frozen green peas, thawed
¼ cup chopped fresh parsley
Salt and freshly ground pepper to taste

1   Heat the oil in a soup pot. Add the onions and sauté over medium-low heat until translucent. Add the garlic and continue to sauté until both are golden.

2   Add the carrots, celery and leaves, potatoes, and just enough water to cover. Stir in the tomatoes, tomato sauce, optional wine, and Italian seasoning. Bring to a slow boil, then lower the heat. Simmer gently over low heat with the cover ajar until the vegetables are just done, about 20 to 25 minutes.

3   Add the chickpeas, green peas, and parsley. Adjust the consistency with more water, as needed, if the broth is too crowded.

4   Season with salt and pepper and simmer over low heat for 10 minutes longer, or until the vegetables are completely tender but not overdone. Serve at once.

MACARONI & CHEESE SOUP

A soothing bowlful in a base of pureed white beans   6 to 8 servings

---

*Here's a favorite nursery food converted into a
mild, cheesy, high-protein soup.*

1 ½ tablespoons vegan butter or olive oil
1 large onion, finely chopped
2 medium celery stalks, finely diced
3 to 3 ½ cups cooked or two 15-ounce cans
   cannellini beans, drained and rinsed
2 cups water
1 vegetable bouillon cube
1 ½ teaspoons salt-free seasoning
   (see page 8 for brands)
1 teaspoon dry mustard
½ teaspoon dried dill
2 cups unsweetened plant-based
   milk, or more, as needed
1 ½ cups cheddar-style vegan cheese shreds
1 cup frozen green peas
2 cups small pasta, such as shells or elbows
Salt and freshly ground pepper to taste

1 Heat the vegan butter in a soup pot. Add the
onion and celery and sauté over medium-low heat
until both are golden.

2 Puree the beans in a blender or food processor
with a small amount of water until smooth.

3 Stir in the bean puree, water, bouillon cube,
salt-free seasoning, mustard, and dill. Bring to a
slow boil, then lower the heat. Simmer gently over
low heat with the cover ajar for 20 to 25 minutes.

4 Stir in enough plant-based milk to give the soup
a slightly thick consistency. Bring the soup to a gentle simmer once again.

5 Sprinkle in the cheese a little at a time, stirring
it in until fairly well melted. Add the peas, remove
from the heat, and cover.

6 In a separate saucepan, cook the pasta until *al
dente*. Drain well and stir into the soup.

7 Adjust the consistency of the soup with more
plant-based milk as needed for a slightly thick consistency. Season with salt and pepper, and serve.

ITALIAN PASTA & BEAN SOUP

The well-loved *pasta e fagioli* with zucchini

*Like Minestrone, this is an Italian standard.
Serve it with Bruschetta (page 25) or fresh
garlic bread.*

2 tablespoons extra-virgin olive oil
1 medium onion, finely chopped
2 cloves garlic, minced
1 medium carrot, peeled and
    cut into ¼-inch dice
1 large celery stalk, cut into ¼-inch dice
3 to 3 ½ cups cooked or two 15-ounce cans
    cannellini beans (drained and rinsed)
6 cups water
2 vegetable bouillon cubes
1 medium zucchini, diced
1 ½ teaspoons Italian seasoning
¼ cup tomato paste
1 ½ cups ditalini (tiny tubular pasta)
Whole oregano leaves and/or chopped
    fresh parsley as desired
Salt and freshly ground pepper to taste

1   Heat the oil in a soup pot. Add the onion, garlic, carrot, and celery, and sauté over medium-low heat, stirring frequently, until all are golden.

2   Add the beans, water, bouillon cubes, zucchini, Italian seasoning, and tomato paste. Bring to a slow boil, then lower the heat. Simmer gently over low heat with the cover ajar until the zucchini is just tender, about 10 minutes. Remove from the heat and allow the soup to stand for an hour or so to develop flavor.

3   Meanwhile, cook the pasta until *al dente* in a separate saucepan. Stir into the soup.

4   Reheat the soup just before serving. Adjust the consistency with more water if the broth is crowded. Stir in the fresh herb, season with salt and pep-

ITALIAN MIXED VEGETABLE STEW

With hearty potato gnocchi   8 or more servings

Gnocchi (Italian dumplings made of semolina and potato flours) add heft to this flavorful stew. Look for them in the frozen food aisle of well-stocked supermarkets near ravioli, tortellini, and other Italian specialties. It isn't difficult to find gnocchi made without eggs, but read labels to make sure. Serve with Bruschetta (page 25) and a green salad embellished with olives and chickpeas.

2 tablespoons extra-virgin olive oil
1 large onion, chopped
3 cloves garlic, minced
2 medium potatoes, peeled and diced
2 cups cut green beans (fresh or frozen)
14.5-ounce can Italian-style diced tomatoes
14.5-ounce can pureed or crushed tomatoes
¼ cup dry red wine, optional
2 teaspoons Italian seasoning
½ teaspoon dried basil
2 cups water
3 heaping cups cauliflower, cut
    into bite-size pieces
1 medium zucchini, quartered
    lengthwise and sliced
16-ounce package frozen
    gnocchi, mostly thawed
Salt and freshly ground pepper to taste

1 Heat the oil in a soup pot. Add the onion and sauté over medium-low heat until translucent. Add the garlic and continue to sauté until both are golden.

2 Add the potatoes, green beans, diced and pureed tomatoes, optional wine, Italian seasoning, and basil. Stir in the water. Bring to a slow boil, then lower the heat. Simmer gently over low heat with the cover ajar until the vegetables are just tender, about 15 minutes.

3 Add the cauliflower and zucchini and cook for 10 to 15 minutes longer, or until all the vegetables are done, but not overcooked.

4 Meanwhile, cook the gnocchi separately in a roomy pot according to package directions. Most take about 10 minutes. When done, drain and gently stir into the stew.

5 Season with salt and pepper and stir in half of the parsley. Add a bit more water if needed, but let the stew remain nice and thick.

6 Serve at once. Top each serving with a sprinkling of the remaining parsley.

CHICK'N NOODLE SOUP

Kind of like my mom's, but without the bird

6 to 8 servings

Vegan chick'n noodle soup conjures up a soup from my childhood (and maybe it will do the same for you). This one proves that cool-weather soups need not always be thick or creamy to provide a sense of coziness. This recipe offers a choice of plant proteins. Because the noodles absorb the broth as the soup stands, it thickens quite a bit. So while it doesn't seem like it makes a lot at first, it keeps on giving. When adding more water to the soup, adjust the seasonings as well.

1 tablespoon olive oil

3 large celery stalks, finely diced

3 medium carrots, peeled and thinly sliced,
   or 1 to 1 ½ cups chopped baby carrots

2 to 3 cloves garlic, minced

1 medium onion, finely chopped

8 cups water

2 vegetable or vegan chick'n-
   style bouillon cubes

1 teaspoon salt-free seasoning
   (see page 8 for brands)

2 cups tiny pasta (see Note)

6 to 8 ounces vegan chick'n product,
   chick'n-style seitan, or baked
   tofu, chopped small pieces

Salt and freshly ground pepper to taste

¼ cup finely chopped fresh parsley

2 to 3 tablespoons chopped fresh dill

1 Heat the oil in a large soup pot. Add the celery, carrots, garlic, onion, and about 2 tablespoons of water. Cover and sweat over medium heat for about 8 minutes, or until the vegetables begin to soften, stirring occasionally.

2 Add the water, bouillon cubes, seasoning, and and bring to a slow boil. Bring to a slow boil, then lower the heat. Simmer gently over low heat with the cover ajar for 15 minutes.

3 Raise the heat and bring to a more vigorous simmer. Add the noodles and vegan chick'n and simmer steadily for 5 to 8 minutes, or until the noodles are *al dente*. Make sure not to overcook, as the noodles will continue to soften in the hot broth.

4 Season with salt and pepper. Stir in the parsley and dill, then serve.

NOTES Anellini is the name for tiny pasta rings. These work great and cook quickly. You can also use vermicelli or angel hair pasta, broken into 1 ½-inch pieces. Or, if you find any other short fine noodles, just make sure they're not egg noodles.

As the soup stands, the noodles quickly absorb the broth. If you plan on reheating any leftover soup, add a cup or so of water before storing, and adjust the seasonings. This way the soup can develop more flavor as it stands.

CHICK'N WILD RICE SOUP

An American classic goes plant-based

Plant-based chick'n or baked tofu are teamed with vegetables and hearty wild rice in this comforting, mild soup. Although wild rice features prominently in the original version of this classic soup, you can swap in brown and wild rice blend, or even forbidden (black) rice.

¾ cup wild rice

3 ½ cups water

1 tablespoon olive oil

1 large onion, finely chopped

3 celery stalks, diced

4 medium carrots, peeled and sliced

6 to 8 ounces mushrooms, any variety, cleaned, stemmed, and sliced

6 cups water

2 vegetable bouillon cubes

2 teaspoons vegan poultry seasoning or salt-free seasoning (see page 8 for brands)

8 to 10 ounces plant-based chick'n or baked tofu, cut into small bite-size pieces

¼ cup quick-cooking oats (oatmeal)

2 cups unsweetened plant-based milk, or more, as needed

Salt and freshly ground pepper to taste

½ cup chopped fresh parsley or cilantro

1 Combine the wild rice with the water in a small saucepan. Bring to a slow boil, then lower the heat and simmer gently with the cover ajar until the water is absorbed, about 35 minutes. It might be still a bit firm at this point, but will cook further in the soup. You can do this step ahead of time.

2 Heat the oil in a large soup pot. Add the onion and sauté over medium-low heat until golden.

3 Add the celery, carrots, mushrooms, water, bouillon cubes, seasoning, and plant-based chick'n. Bring to a slow boil, then lower the heat. Simmer gently over low heat with the cover ajar for 20 minutes.

4 Add the cooked wild rice, oats, and plant-based milk. Add more plant-based milk if the soup is too dense.

5 Season with salt and pepper and simmer gently for 10 minutes longer. Stir in the parsley and serve.

CELERY, POTATO & MUSHROOM SOUP

An everyday soup with winter vegetables and barley or farro 6 servings

This is just the sort of simple, mild soup that hits the spot on winter days. Quick Sunflower-Cheese Bread (page 18) is an excellent accompaniment.

2 tablespoons olive oil

1 large onion, chopped

2 tablespoons unbleached white flour

5 cups water

2 vegetable bouillon cubes

4 large celery stalks, diced

A handful of celery leaves, chopped

3 medium potatoes, diced

⅓ cup raw pearl barley or farro

8 ounces mushrooms, any variety, cleaned, stemmed, and coarsely chopped

2 teaspoons salt-free seasoning (see page 8 for brands)

1 cup frozen green peas, thawed

1 ½ to 2 cups unsweetened plant-based milk, or more, as needed

Salt and freshly ground pepper to taste

1 Heat the oil in a soup pot. Add the onion and sauté over medium-low heat until golden.

2 Sprinkle in the flour, a little at a time, and stir in. Slowly stir in about 1 cup of the water, then add the remaining water with bouillon cubes, celery, celery leaves, potatoes, and barley. Bring to a slow boil, then lower the heat and simmer gently over low heat with the cover ajar for 15 minutes.

3 Add the mushrooms and seasoning. Continue to simmer gently until the barley is tender, about 25 to 30 minutes longer.

4 Add the peas and enough plant-based milk to give the soup a medium-thick consistency.

5 Season with salt and pepper, and simmer over very low heat for 10 minutes longer. This soup thickens as it stands; thin any leftovers with additional water or plant-based milk, then taste to adjust the seasonings.

MIXED MUSHROOM BARLEY SOUP

The classic combo with a farro variation

In its basic form, mushroom barley soup is a great comfort classic. In this version, using a variety of mushrooms adds interest. You also have the option of making it a mushroom-farro soup by swapping in this nutty ancient grain. Whether you use pearled barley or farro, this isn't a quick-cooking soup, so make it when you're not in a hurry. It's a good soup to make on a chilly Sunday afternoon and enjoy for dinner later in the day and then for the first part of the week. This soup thickens a lot as it stands, so there may be plenty of leftovers!

2 tablespoons olive oil

1 large or 2 medium onions, finely chopped

2 to 3 cloves garlic, minced

1 cup raw pearl barley (or pearled or semi-pearled farro)

3 large celery stalks, diced

2 medium carrots, peeled and thinly sliced

8 cups water with 2 vegetable bouillon cubes

1 tablespoon salt-free seasoning (see page 8 for brands)

1 teaspoon curry powder or ¼ teaspoon turmeric (for color, optional)

12 to 16 ounces mushrooms, stemmed and sliced (use a combination of any two or three; see Note for varieties)

2 cups unsweetened plant-based milk, more or less as needed

½ cup chopped fresh parsley (or ¼ cup each chopped fresh parsley and dill)

Salt and freshly ground pepper to taste

1 Heat the oil in a soup pot. Add the onions and sauté over medium-low heat until translucent. Add the garlic and continue to sauté until both are golden.

2 Add the barley, celery, carrot, vegetable broth, water, salt-free seasoning, and optional curry powder. Bring to a slow boil, then lower the heat. Simmer gently over low heat with the cover ajar for 30 minutes.

3 Stir in the mushrooms and simmer for 20 to 30 minutes longer, or until the barley and vegetables are tender.

4 Add enough plant-based milk to give the soup a slightly thick consistency. Stir in the parsley (or parsley/dill combination), and season with salt and pepper.

5 If time allows, let the soup stand for an hour or so off the heat. Just before serving, heat the soup through; Add more plant-based milk as needed, and adjust the seasonings.

NOTE I recommend using a combination of cremini (aka baby bella) mushrooms and one or two other varieties. Good choices include shiitakes (fresh, or dried and rehydrated), oyster mushrooms, and portobellos.

PARSNIP VEGETABLE BISQUE

A trio of root vegetables in a creamy tomato base

Here's a soothing, mild soup for cold weather.
This is delicious with Garlic Croutons (page 25).

1 ½ tablespoons olive oil
1 ½ cups chopped onion
1 large celery stalk, diced
Handful of celery leaves
1 pound parsnips, scraped and
    cut into ½-inch dice
2 large potatoes, peeled and
    cut into ½-inch dice
2 medium carrots, peeled and
    coarsely chopped
14.5-ounce can diced tomatoes
2 teaspoons salt-free seasoning
    (see page 8 for brands)
2 vegetable bouillon cubes
¼ cup chopped fresh parsley
2 cups unsweetened plant-based
    milk, or more, as needed
Salt and freshly ground pepper to taste
Croutons for serving, optional
Vegan sour cream (homemade, page 7,
    or from an 8-ounce tub), optional

1 Heat the oil in a soup pot. Add the onion and celery and sauté over medium-low heat until both are golden.

2 Add the celery leaves, parsnips, potatoes, carrots, tomatoes, seasoning, bouillon cubes, and just enough water to barely cover the vegetables. Bring to a slow boil, then lower the heat. Simmer gently over low heat with the cover ajar until the vegetables are tender, about 20 to 30 minutes. Remove from the heat.

3 With a slotted spoon, transfer half of the vegetables to a food processor or blender. Process until smoothly pureed, then stir back into the soup. Or, skip the food processor and insert an immersion blender into the soup pot; process until about half of the soup is pureed.

4 Stir in the parsley and enough plant-based milk to give the soup a slightly thick consistency. Season with salt and pepper. Return the soup to low heat and simmer very gently for 5 to 10 minutes, or until piping hot.

5 Serve at once with optional croutons and/or sour cream. This soup thickens as it stands. Thin the consistency of any leftover soup with additional plant-based milk, and adjust the seasonings.

HEARTY WINTER ROOTS SOUP

A medley of chunky root vegetables with a hint of cheese 6 to 8 servings

This hearty soup makes use of a pair of humble winter vegetables—parsnips and rutabaga—to great effect. Make sure to use a good, sharp knife to cut the rutabaga.

2 tablespoons olive oil
1 large onion, chopped
2 to 3 cloves garlic, minced
1 large or 2 medium rutabaga,
    peeled and diced
2 medium carrots, peeled and
    coarsely chopped
2 medium potatoes, scrubbed and diced
2 medium parsnips, peeled and diced
1 large celery stalk, diced
⅓ cup quick-cooking oats
¼ cup dry white wine, optional
2 teaspoons salt-free seasoning
    (see page 8 for brands)
2 vegetable bouillon cubes
1 cup unsweetened plant-based
    milk, or more, as needed
1 cup cheddar-style vegan cheese shreds
Salt and freshly ground pepper to taste

1 Heat the oil in a soup pot. Add the onion and sauté over medium-low heat until translucent. Add the garlic and continue to sauté until both are golden.

2 Add the rutabaga, carrots, potatoes, parsnips, celery, oats, optional wine, salt-free seasoning, bouillon cubes, and enough water to barely cover the vegetables. Bring to a slow boil, then lower the heat. Simmer gently over low heat with the cover ajar until the vegetables are tender, about 25 to 30 minutes.

3 With a slotted spoon, remove about 2 cups of the vegetables and transfer to a shallow bowl or a plate. Mash coarsely, then stir back into the soup. Add the plant-based milk and allow the soup to simmer over very low heat for 10 minutes longer.

4 Sprinkle the cheese in a little at a time, stirring it in until fairly well melted.

5 If the soup is too thick, adjust the consistency with more plant-based milk. Season with salt and pepper. Serve at once, or if time allows, let the soup stand off the heat for an hour or so, then reheat as needed before serving.

ESCAROLE, POTATO & WHITE BEAN SOUP

An under-appreciated leafy green in a simple, tasty soup   6 servings

A warming choice for a chilly winter day, this soup is inspired by a classic Italian recipe. It's a fantastic way to enjoy escarole, an often overlooked leafy green that looks like romaine lettuce, but a bit darker. Slightly bitter when uncooked, it mellows beautifully in the soup.

2 tablespoons extra virgin olive oil

1 medium onion, quartered and thinly sliced

2 to 3 cloves garlic, minced

6 medium or 4 large potatoes, any
   variety, peeled and diced

2 medium carrots, thinly sliced

32-ounce carton vegetable broth or 4 cups
   water with 2 vegetable bouillon cubes

1 teaspoon dried basil

½ teaspoon dried thyme

15-ounce can cannellini beans,
   drained and rinsed

1 head escarole (6 to 8 ounces),
   coarsely chopped and well rinsed

½ cup chopped fresh parsley

Salt and freshly ground pepper to taste

1 Heat the oil in a soup pot. Add the onion and sauté over medium-low heat until translucent. Add the garlic and continue to sauté until both are golden.

2 Add the potatoes, carrots, broth, basil, thyme, and 2 cups water. Bring to a slow boil, then lower the heat. Simmer gently over low heat with the cover ajar for 20 minutes, or until the potatoes and carrots are tender.

3 Stir in the beans, escarole, and half of the parsley. Simmer gently for 8 to 10 minutes, or until the escarole is tender.

4 With the back of a wooden spoon or a potato masher, mash some of the potatoes in the soup to thicken the base. Stir in water as needed (up to 2 cups). The soup should be thick, but not overly crowded. Return to a simmer.

5 Stir in the remaining parsley, then season with salt and pepper. If time allows, let the soup stand off the heat for an hour or more before serving. Adjust the consistency and seasonings, then reheat.

VARIATIONS This is also good with kale, chard, or broccoli rabe. Use equivalent amounts; stem and chop the kale and chard; cut broccoli rabe into ½-inch segments.

CHICKPEA & BULGUR STEW

A tasty grain-and-bean combo with winter vegetables

6 to 8 servings

Bulgur isn't often used in soups, but works quite nicely, adding a subtly nutty flavor and chewy texture.

1 ½ tablespoons olive oil

1 large onion, chopped

2 to 3 cloves garlic, minced

2 large celery stalks, diced

32-ounce carton vegetable broth or 4 cups
   water with 2 vegetable bouillon cubes

2 medium white turnips, peeled and diced

½ cup finely shredded cabbage

½ cup raw bulgur

28-ounce can fire roasted or
   Italian diced tomatoes

2 teaspoons Italian seasoning

2 teaspoons sweet paprika

15-ounce can chickpeas, drained and rinsed

Salt and freshly ground pepper to taste

¼ cup chopped fresh parsley,
   or more, to taste

1 Heat the the oil in a large soup pot. Add the onion and sauté over medium-low heat until translucent. Add the garlic and celery and continue to sauté until all are golden.

2 Add the broth, turnips, cabbage, bulgur, tomatoes, Italian seasoning, and paprika. Bring to a slow boil, then lower the heat. Simmer gently over low heat with the cover ajar for 30 to 35 minutes, or until the bulgur and vegetables are tender.

3 Add the chickpeas, then season with salt and pepper. Simmer over very low heat for 10 minutes longer.

4 If time allows, let the soup stand off the heat for about an hour to develop flavor. Add a bit more water if needed, adjust the seasonings, and then reheat as needed. Stir the parsley into the soup just before serving.

SWEET & SOUR CABBAGE SOUP

A hearty bowlful for a blustery winter day

6 servings

Here's a variation of classic sweet-and-sour cabbage soup, given a bit more heft with the addition of bread cubes in each bowl.

**3 to 4 cups cubed (about 1 inch)
  Italian or sourdough bread**
2 tablespoons olive oil
**1 large or 2 medium onions,
  quartered and thinly sliced**
3 to 4 cloves garlic, minced
5 cups water
**2 large or 3 medium carrots,
  peeled and sliced**
**2 large or 3 medium potatoes,
  cut into ½-inch dice**
4 cups coarsely shredded green cabbage
1 medium green or red bell pepper, diced
**14.5-ounce can fire roasted or
  Italian-style diced tomatoes**
¼ cup dry red wine, optional
2 teaspoons sweet paprika
½ teaspoon ground cumin
3 tablespoons lemon juice, or to taste
**3 tablespoons natural granulated
  sugar, or to taste**
Salt and freshly ground pepper to taste

1 Preheat the oven to 300° F. Spread the bread cubes in a single layer on a baking sheet and bake until golden and crisp, about 12 to 15 minutes. Remove from the oven and set aside.

2 Heat the oil in a soup pot. Add the onion and sauté over medium-low heat until translucent. Add the garlic and continue to sauté until both are golden.

3 Add the water, carrots, potatoes, cabbage, bell pepper, tomatoes, optional wine, paprika, and cumin. Bring to a slow boil, then lower the heat. Simmer gently over low heat with the cover ajar for 25 to 30 minutes, or until the vegetables are tender.

4 Stir in the lemon juice and sugar. There should be a subtle sweet-sour balance. If you'd like it to be more pronounced, add more lemon juice and/or sugar to your liking.

5 Season with salt and pepper, then simmer over very low heat for 10 minutes longer. If time allows, let the soup stand off the heat for an hour or two to develop flavor. Add a little more water if needed, and adjust the seasonings and sweet-sour balance. Reheat before serving.

6 Serve in one of two ways: Either divide the bread cubes among the serving bowls and ladle the soup over them; the bread will absorb much of the liquid and add a tasty, textural element to the soup. Or, pass around the bread cubes to use as croutons.

SPANISH GARBANZO STEW

Well-seasoned chickpeas with tomatoes, garlic, and parsley   6 to 8 servings

This classic recipe is easy and quick to prepare. Accompany with crusty fresh bread, or serve or atop a bed of rice or other grain.

1 ½ tablespoons extra-virgin olive oil
1 large onion, chopped
3 to 4 cloves garlic, minced
1 large green bell pepper, cut
   into short narrow strips
2 cups water
3 to 3 ½ cups cooked chickpeas, or two
   15-ounce cans, drained and rinsed
28-ounce can fire roasted diced tomatoes
1 teaspoon ground cumin
1 teaspoon dried oregano
¼ teaspoon dried thyme
¼ cup chopped fresh cilantro or parsley
Salt and freshly ground pepper to taste

1   Heat the oil in a large soup pot. Add the onion and sauté over medium-low heat until translucent. Add the garlic and green pepper and continue to sauté until all are golden.

2   Add the water, chickpeas, tomatoes, cumin, oregano, and thyme. Bring to a slow boil, then lower the heat. Simmer gently over low heat with the cover ajar for 20 minutes.

3   Stir in the parsley and season with salt and pepper. Adjust the consistency with more water if needed, but let the stew remain thick. Serve at once.

GOLDEN CURRIED PEA SOUP

The stick-to-your-ribs classic, gently curried

8 or more servings

On frigid days, this thick, long-simmering classic winter soup is a natural choice as a hearty main dish. It's delicious served with Garlic Croutons (page 25) and a simple salad or slaw.

2 tablespoons olive oil
1 large or 2 medium onions, finely chopped
2 medium carrots, peeled and diced
2 to 3 cloves garlic, crushed or minced
8 cups water
2 vegetable bouillon cubes
1 pound dried yellow split peas, rinsed
⅓ cup raw brown rice or barley, rinsed
2 teaspoons good-quality curry
   powder, more or less to taste
½ teaspoon turmeric
1 teaspoon grated fresh or bottled ginger
Pinch of nutmeg
Salt and freshly ground pepper to taste

1 Heat the oil in a soup pot. Add the onion and sauté over medium-low heat until golden.

2 Add all the remaining ingredients except the salt and pepper. Bring to a slow boil, then lower the heat. Simmer gently over low heat with the cover ajar until the peas are mushy, about 1 ½ hours, stirring occasionally.

3 When the peas are done, adjust the consistency with more water if needed, but let the soup stay nice and thick. Season with salt and pepper, then serve. This soup thickens considerably as it stands; thin with additional water, as needed, and adjust the seasonings.

PROVENÇAL BEAN STEW

A wine-scented stew featuring navy beans

6 servings

This meatless version of a rustic Provençal stew is aromatic and satisfying. A fresh, crusty French baguette is perfect for soaking up the flavorful broth. A colorful tossed salad makes it a complete meal.

2 tablespoons extra-virgin olive oil

1 large onion, chopped

3 to 4 cloves garlic, minced

2 cups water

2 medium carrots, peeled and sliced

4 celery stalks, diced

½ cup dry red wine, optional

3 to 3 ½ cups cooked navy beans, or two 15-ounce cans, drained and rinsed

14.5-ounce can diced tomatoes

½ teaspoon dried thyme

1 teaspoon minced fresh rosemary or ½ teaspoon dried, or more to taste

Salt and freshly ground pepper to taste

½ cup chopped fresh parsley

1 Heat the oil in a soup pot. Add the onion and sauté over medium-low heat until translucent. Add the garlic and continue to sauté until both are golden.

2 Add the water, carrots, celery, and wine. Bring to a slow boil, then lower the heat. Simmer gently over low heat with the cover ajar for 10 minutes.

3 Stir in the beans, tomatoes, thyme, and rosemary. Continue to cook for 15 to 20 minutes. If needed, add a small amount of additional water. The consistency should be thick and not too soupy.

4 Stir in half of the parsley. Season with salt and pepper and serve. Sprinkle the remaining parsley over each serving.

VARIATION To make this an even heartier dish, add vegan sausage. Cut 4 links into ½-inch thick slices. Sauté them in a small amount of olive oil over medium heat until golden brown here and there, stirring often. Stir the vegan sausage into the stew once it's done.

LONG-SIMMERING BLACK BEAN SOUP

Robust and bursting with flavor   8 or more servings

If you're stuck inside during a snowstorm, making this soup is an ideal activity! While it's cooking, make Cheese and Herb Corn Muffins (page 21) or Green Chili Cornbread (page 24) to serve with it.

1 pound dried black beans, rinsed
1 large onion, chopped
3 medium carrots, peeled and sliced
2 large celery stalks, diced
3 to 4 cloves garlic, minced
2 teaspoons salt-free seasoning
   (see page 8 for brands)
2 teaspoons smoked paprika
   or barbecue seasoning
¼ cup dry red wine or sherry, optional
¼ cup chopped fresh cilantro or
   parsley, plus more for garnish
Juice of ½ to 1 lemon or lime, to taste
Salt and freshly ground pepper to taste
Peeled and diced avocado
   for garnish, optional

1 Soak the beans overnight in a large soup pot with plenty of water, covered and refrigerated. Alternatively, cover the beans with water in a soup pot, bring to a boil, then let stand off the heat for an hour or two.

2 In either case, drain the beans after soaking, and rinse. Place in a soup pot with fresh water in a ratio of approximately 3 parts water to 1 part beans. Bring to a slow boil, then lower the heat. Simmer gently over low heat with the cover ajar for 1 hour.

3 Add the onion, carrots, celery, garlic, seasoning, smoked paprika, and optional wine. Simmer for 1 to 1 ½ hours, or until the beans are soft. You should be able to easily press a bean between your thumb and forefinger.

4 Scoop out about 1 ½ cups of the beans with a slotted spoon, avoiding scooping out the other vegetables as much as possible. Set aside.

5 Transfer the solid ingredients, in batches, to a food processor or blender. Use about ¼ cup of the cooking liquid per batch. Process until smoothly pureed, then return the puree to the soup pot along with the reserved beans. Or, skip the food processor and insert an immersion blender into the pot and blend the soup until pureed to your liking.

6 Stir in the cilantro and lemon juice, then season with salt and pepper. Simmer gently for 10 minutes.

7 To serve, top each bowlful with more cilantro and optional diced avocado.

BRAZILIAN BLACK BEAN STEW

A beautiful bowl of black beans, sweet potatoes, and rice   6 to 8 servings

A vegetarian version of Brazil's famous national dish, feijoada, *this stew is abundant with nourishing ingredients. Serve with steamed fresh greens (you can sauté them with garlic in olive oil) and slices of mango and/or papaya.*

For the rice
1 cup tomato juice or tomato sauce
3 cups water
1 ½ cups raw brown rice, rinsed

For the stew
1 tablespoon olive oil
1 large onion, chopped
2 cloves garlic, minced
2 medium sweet potatoes, peeled and diced
1 ½ cups water
3 to 3 ½ cups cooked black beans, or two
    15-ounce cans, drained and rinsed
1 medium red bell pepper, cut
    into short, narrow strips
1 medium green or yellow bell pepper,
    cut into short, narrow strips
1 cup diced ripe tomatoes
2 small fresh hot green chili peppers,
    seeded and thinly sliced, divided
1 ½ teaspoons ground cumin
½ teaspoon dried thyme
½ cup chopped fresh parsley or cilantro
Salt and freshly ground pepper to taste

1   Combine the tomato juice with the water in a large saucepan and bring to a slow boil. Add the rice, then lower the heat and simmer gently with the cover ajar until all the liquid is absorbed and the rice is tender, about 30 minutes. Cover and set the cooked rice aside until needed.

2   Meanwhile, heat the oil in a large soup pot. Add the onion and sauté over medium-low heat until translucent. Add the garlic and continue to sauté until both are golden.

3   Stir in the sweet potatoes and water. Bring to a slow boil, then lower the heat. Simmer gently over low heat with the cover ajar until the sweet potatoes are just tender but still firm, about 10 to 15 minutes.

4   Add the beans, bell peppers, tomatoes, one of the chili peppers, cumin, and thyme. Simmer gently for 10 to 15 minutes longer, uncovered. The stew should have the consistency of a thick chili—nice and moist, but not overly soupy. Add a bit more water if too thick.

5   Stir in half of the parsley and season with salt and pepper. Serve over the hot cooked rice in shallow bowls, and garnish each serving with a little of the extra parsley and a few slices of the reserved chili pepper.

THYME-SCENTED TOMATO RICE SOUP

A sturdy, fragrant soup for chilly nights

6 to 8 servings

Tomato and brown rice soup features a classic pairing of ingredients that are just made for each other, enhanced with the fragrance of fresh thyme.

1 ½ tablespoons olive oil

1 large onion, chopped

2 to 3 cloves garlic, minced

1 large celery stalk, diced

2 medium carrots, peeled and sliced

28-ounce can diced tomatoes
   (try fire-roasted)

½ cup finely chopped sun-dried
   tomatoes (see note)

¾ cup raw brown rice, any variety, rinsed

1 large or 2 regular vegetable bouillon cubes

2 teaspoons salt-free seasoning
   (see page 8 for brands)

6 cups water

Leaves from several sprigs fresh
   thyme (about 2 teaspoons),
   plus more for garnish

Salt and freshly ground pepper to taste

1   Heat the oil in a soup pot. Add the onion and sauté over medium-low heat until translucent. Add the garlic and continue to sauté until both are golden.

2   Add the remaining ingredients except the thyme garnish, salt, and pepper. Bring to a slow boil, then lower the heat. Simmer gently over low heat with the cover ajar for 45 minutes, stirring every 15 minutes or so, or until the rice is tender.

3   The soup should have a medium-thick consistnecy. If too thick, adjust the consistency with more water as needed, and return to a gentle simmer. Season with salt and pepper.

4   Serve at once, or if time allows, let the soup stand off the heat for an hour or so. This soup thickens quite a bit as it stands. Add water and adjust the seasonings, as needed, before reheating and serving.

THREE BEAN SOUP WITH BROWN RICE

Red, white, and green beans in a tomato broth   8 servings

This warming, high-fiber soup, makes a hearty centerpiece served with Green Chili Cornbread (page 24) and a simple coleslaw.

2 tablespoons olive oil

1 large onion, chopped

2 to 3 cloves garlic, minced

1 large celery stalk, diced

6 cups water

½ cup raw brown rice, rinsed

14.5-ounce can crushed tomatoes

1 ½ teaspoons dried oregano

1 teaspoon chili powder

2 heaping cups frozen green beans, thawed

15-ounce can Great Northern or
    cannellini beans, drained and rinsed

15-ounce can kidney or red
    beans, drained and rinsed

1 tablespoon lime juice, or more to taste

¼ cup chopped fresh cilantro or parsley

Salt and freshly ground pepper to taste

Thinly sliced limes wedges
    for garnish, optional

1 Heat the oil in a soup pot. Add the onion and sauté over medium-low heat until translucent. Add the garlic and celery and continue to sauté until all are golden.

2 Add the water, rice, tomatoes, oregano, and chili powder. Bring to a slow boil, then lower the heat. Simmer gently over low heat with the cover ajar for 30 minutes.

3 Add the three types of beans and simmer over very low heat for 15 to 20 minutes longer, or until the rice and green beans are tender.

4 Stir in the lime juice and cilantro, then season with salt and pepper. If time allows, let the soup stand off the heat for an hour or more, then heat through before serving. Garnish each serving with two or three lime wedges, if desired.

THAI-SPICED SWEET POTATO STEW

Nourishing sweet potatoes in a delectable coconut base

6 servings

Now that Thai ingredients available at most natural foods stores and well-stocked supermarkets, it has become easy to enjoy the delightful flavors of this cuisine at home. Adding the optional baked tofu or plant based chick'n will make this main dish stew even heartier.

1 tablespoon olive oil
1 medium onion, quartered and thinly sliced
4 to 6 cloves garlic, minced
3 medium-large sweet potatoes (about
  1 ½ pounds), peeled and diced
3 cups water
1 medium bell pepper, any color,
  cut into narrow strips
1 ½ cups frozen green beans
2 teaspoons grated fresh or bottled ginger
13.5-ounce can light coconut milk
2 tablespoons natural peanut butter
8-ounce package baked tofu or plant-
  based chick'n, chopped, optional
Salt and freshly ground pepper to taste
Sriracha sauce or other hot
  seasoning to taste
Cilantro leaves for garnish

1   Heat the oil in a soup pot. Add the onion and sauté over medium-low heat until translucent. Add the garlic and continue to sauté until both are golden.

2   Add the sweet potatoes and water. Bring to a slow boil, then lower the heat. Simmer gently over low heat with the cover ajar for 10 minutes, or until the sweet potatoes are about half done.

3   Add the bell pepper, green beans, and ginger. Simmer for 10 minutes longer.

4   Stir in the coconut milk, peanut butter, and optional tofu. Return to a simmer, then cook over very low heat for 10 minutes, or until all the vegetables are tender.

5   Season with salt, pepper, and sriracha (go easy, as it can be passed around for individual portions). Taste to adjust the other seasonings.

6   Serve at once. Garnish each serving with a few cilantro leaves.

HEARTY BARLEY BEAN SOUP

A main dish soup featuring nourishing grains and beans

This is a basic, everyday sort of soup, an economical way to warm up. Try Cheese and Herb Corn Muffins (page 21) as an accompaniment.

2 tablespoons olive oil

2 large onions, chopped

2 to 3 cloves garlic, minced

6 cups water

¾ cup raw pearl or pot barley, rinsed

2 large celery stalks, diced

Handful of celery leaves

2 medium carrots, peeled and sliced

2 ½ teaspoons salt-free seasoning
   (see page 8 for brands)

14.5-ounce can diced tomatoes

15-ounce can kidney, red, or pink
   beans, drained and rinsed

¼ cup chopped fresh parsley

2 tablespoons minced fresh dill

Salt and freshly ground pepper to taste

1 Heat the oil in a soup pot. Add the onions and sauté over medium-low heat until translucent. Add the garlic and continue to sauté until both are golden.

2 Add the water, barley, celery, celery leaves, carrots, salt-free seasoning, and tomatoes. Bring to a slow boil, then lower the heat. Simmer gently over low heat with the cover ajar for 45 minutes, or until the barley and vegetables are tender.

3 Add the beans, parsley, and dill. Season with salt and pepper, then simmer for 10 to 15 minutes longer over low heat.

4 Serve at once, or if time allows, let the soup stand off the heat for an hour or so. The soup thickens as it stands. Add water, as needed, and adjust the seasonings, then reheat before serving.

TOMATO, LENTIL & BARLEY SOUP

A high-protein, everyday main-dish soup

6 to 8 servings

Lentil soups are so satisfying when the winter winds are blowing. Served with Quick Sunflower Cheese Bread (page 18) or Focaccia (page 22), this soup needs only a simple salad to make a filling meal.

1 tablespoon olive oil
1 large onion, chopped
2 to 3 cloves garlic, minced
6 cups water
8 ounces raw brown or green lentils, rinsed
¾ cup raw pearl or pot barley, rinsed
2 large celery stalks, diced
2 medium carrots, peeled and sliced
1 cup shredded green cabbage
28-ounce can diced tomatoes
¼ cup dry red wine, optional
1 to 2 tablespoons apple cider
   vinegar, to taste
¼ cup chopped fresh parsley
2 teaspoons salt-free seasoning
   (see page 8 for brands)
2 teaspoons paprika
Salt and freshly ground pepper to taste

1   Heat the oil in a soup pot. Add the onion and sauté over medium-low heat until translucent. Add the garlic and continue to sauté until both are golden.

2   Add all the remaining ingredients except the salt and pepper. Bring to a slow boil, then lower the heat. Simmer gently over low heat with the cover ajar for 45 to 55 minutes, or until the lentils, barley, and vegetables are tender. Stir occasionally and add more water if the soup becomes too thick.

3   Season with salt and pepper. If time allows, let the soup stand off the heat for an hour or so, then heat through before serving. This soup thickens as it stands; add water, as needed, and adjust the seasonings.

LENTIL, POTATO & CAULIFLOWER SOUP

With spinach and lots of garlic

This soup features a slew of compatible ingredients made even more companionable in a mildly curried broth.

1 ½ tablespoons olive oil

1 large onion, chopped

4 to 6 cloves garlic, minced

1 cup raw brown or green lentils, rinsed

1 large celery stalk, diced

6 cups water

2 large potatoes, scrubbed and diced

14.5-ounce can diced tomatoes

2 teaspoons good-quality curry
    powder, or to taste

½ teaspoon ground turmeric

Pinch of nutmeg

2 ½ cups finely chopped cauliflower pieces

2 to 3 ounces baby spinach

1/4 cup chopped fresh cilantro

Juice of ½ lemon

Salt and freshly ground pepper to taste

1   Heat the oil in a soup pot. Add the onion and sauté over medium-low heat until translucent. Add the garlic and continue to sauté until both are golden.

2   Add the lentils, celery, and water. Bring to a slow boil, then lower the heat. Simmer gently over low heat with the cover ajar for 10 minutes.

3   Add the potatoes, tomatoes, curry powder, turmeric, and nutmeg. Cook until the potatoes are half done, about 10 minutes.

4   Add the cauliflower and continue to cook until the lentils and vegetables are tender, about 20 minutes longer.

5   Stir in the spinach, cilantro, and lemon juice. Adjust the consistency with more water as needed, then season with salt and pepper. Simmer over very low heat for 5 minutes longer.

6   Serve at once, or if time allows, let the soup stand off the heat for an hour or so. Reheat before serving. The soup thickens as it stands. Add water, as needed, and adjust the seasonings.

"BEEFY" SEITAN STEW

Vegan "meat and potatoes" with carrots and green beans   8 servings

Seitan gives this vegetable-filled stew a hearty texture. It's a "beefy" vegan stew that proves you can do without actual meat. As mentioned earlier in this book, my seitan recipe is one of the most popular on the web — search for "easy homemade seitan recipe" at TheVeganAtlas.com.

2 tablespoons olive oil, divided

2 medium or 1 large onion, chopped

2 cloves garlic, minced

3 cups water

5 medium golden or red-skinned
   potatoes, peeled or scrubbed
   and cut into ¾-inch chunks

4 medium carrots, peeled and sliced

1 vegetable bouillon cube

2 teaspoons salt-free seasoning
   (see page 8 for brands)

2 teaspoons sweet paprika

¼ cup dry red wine, optional

2 cups thawed frozencut green beans
   or fresh green beans, trimmed
   and cut into 1-inch lengths

2 tablespoons soy sauce or tamari

1 to 1 ½ pounds packaged or
   homemade seitan (see headnote),
   cut into bite-sized chunks

Salt and freshly ground pepper to taste

¼ cup chopped fresh parsley,
   or more, to taste

1   Heat half of the oil in a large soup pot. Add the onion and sauté over medium-low heat until translucent. Add the garlic and continue to sauté until both are golden.

2   Add the water, potatoes, carrots, bouillon cube, salt-free seasoning, paprika, and optional wine. Bring to a slow boil, then lower the heat. Simmer gently over low heat with the cover ajar for 15 to 20 minutes, or until the potato and carrots are nearly tender.

3   Stir in the green beans and continue to simmer gently.

4   Meanwhile, heat the remaining oil, along with the soy sauce, in a large skillet. Add the seitan pieces and sauté over medium-high heat, stirring frequently, until most sides are nicely browned and crisp, about 10 minutes. Set aside.

5   Once the potatoes in the soup pot are tender, use the back of a wooden spoon to mash enough of them to thicken the base of the stew.

6   Stir in the sautéed seitan. Add a bit more water ,as needed. The consistency should be thick and moist, but not soupy. The vegetables should all be tender by this point, but if they're not, continue to cook for a few minutes longer.

7   Season with salt and pepper (use salt sparingly, if at all, since there are a few salty ingredients). Stir in the parsley and serve.

MISO SOUP WITH WINTER VEGETABLES

Surprisingly substantial, with roots, cabbage, and tofu · 6 servings

Filled with root vegetables, this miso soup is more filling than the more standard recipe. Use your favorite type of miso — Hatcho, mugi, or mellow white miso, my favorite variety for this soup. There's also the new kid on the block, chickpea miso, for those with soy sensitivity.

1 tablespoon olive oil

2 medium onions, quartered and sliced

4 medium potatoes, any variety,
  peeled and diced (see Variations)

1 ½ cups shredded green cabbage,
  preferably napa

1 large celery stalk, cut into
  thick matchsticks

1 large carrot, peeled and cut
  into thick matchsticks

1 cup peeled and diced daikon
  radish, white turnip, or parsnip

6 cups water

2 teaspoons grated fresh or bottled ginger

¼ cup dry red wine or sherry, optional

8 ounces soft or firm tofu, well
  blotted and cut into small dice

2 tablespoons miso, any variety,
  or more, to taste

Freshly ground pepper to taste

1   Heat the oil in a soup pot. Add the onions and sauté over medium-low heat until golden.

2   Add the potatoes, cabbage, celery, carrot, and daikon radish.

3   Add the water, then stir in the ginger and optional wine. Bring to a slow boil, then lower the heat. Simmer gently over low heat with the cover ajar for 20 minutes, or until the vegetables are done.

4   Stir in the tofu. Adjust the consistency with more water if the broth is crowded. Cook for a minute or so longer, then remove from the heat.

5   Dissolve the miso in just enough water to make it smooth and pourable. Stir it into the soup, then taste; repeat the process with more miso if you'd like.

6   Season with plenty of pepper, and serve at once.

VARIATIONS

Substitute one medium sweet potato for two of the regular potatoes.

TACO SOUP

The zesty flavors of tacos turned inside out

The presentation of this easy, offbeat soup is fun and dramatic.

4 cups water, divided
½ cup raw bulgur
1 tablespoon olive oil
1 large onion, chopped
2 to 3 cloves garlic, minced
1 medium green bell pepper, finely diced
3 to 3 ½ cups cooked pinto or pink beans, or
    two 15-ounce cans (drained and rinsed)
28-ounce can crushed tomatoes
¼ cup chopped mild green chilis,
    fresh or canned, optional
¼ cup chopped fresh cilantro, optional
1 to 2 teaspoons chili powder, or to taste
1 teaspoon ground cumin
1 teaspoon dried oregano

Garnishes
1 to 1 ½ cups cheddar or jack-
    style vegan cheese shreds
Thinly shredded romaine or
    green leaf lettuce
Finely diced firm, ripe tomatoes
    (about 1 cup)
Triangular stone-ground tortilla chips

1 Bring 1 cup of the water to a boil in a small saucepan. Add the bulgur and simmer, covered, for 15 minutes, or until the water is absorbed. Or, if you do this step ahead of time, simply add the bulgur to the boiling water, cover, and remove from the heat. Let stand for 30 minutes.

2 Heat the oil in a soup pot. Add the onion and sauté over medium-low heat until translucent. Add the garlic and bell pepper and continue to sauté, stirring frequently, until all are golden.

3 Add the remaining ingredients (other than the garnishes) along with the cooked bulgur and remaining 3 cups of water. Bring to a slow boil, then lower the heat. Simmer gently over low heat with the cover ajar for 10 to 15 minutes, then remove from the heat.

4 Assemble each serving as follows: Fill each bowl about ⅔ full with soup. Divide the cheese, shredded lettuce, and diced tomatoes among them.

5 Line the perimeter of each bowl with several tortilla chips, points facing outward, to create a star-shaped effect. The tortilla chips can be used to scoop up the solid parts of the soup or just nibbled along with the soup. Pass around a bowl of extra tortilla chips.

WHITE BEAN & HOMINY CHILI

A colorful stew featuring sweet potatoes

This offbeat chili is a pleasing introduction to whole hominy. Hominy results from soaking corn kernels until the hulls come off. You'll find canned hominy shelved near other canned corn products on supermarket shelves.

1 tablespoon olive oil

1 large onion, chopped

2 cloves garlic, minced

1 medium red or green bell pepper,
   cut into short narrow strips

1 large or 2 medium sweet
   potatoes, peeled and diced

3 cups water

3 to 3 ½ cups cooked great northern beans
   or two 15-ounce cans, drained and rinsed

15- to 16-ounce can whole
   white or yellow hominy

14.5-ounce can diced tomatoes
   (try fire roasted)

1 cup frozen corn kernels

1 to 2 fresh hot (jalapeño) or mild (poblano)
   chilis, or 1 to 2 chopped canned chipotle
   chilis in adobo sauce (see Note)

2 teaspoons ground cumin

1 teaspoon dried oregano

¼ cup chopped fresh cilantro or parsley

Salt to taste

Dried hot red pepper flakes
   to taste, optional

1 Heat the oil in a large soup pot. Add the onion and sauté over medium-low heat until translucent. Add the garlic and continue to sauté until both are golden.

2 Stir in the bell pepper, sweet potatoes, and water. Bring to a slow boil, then lower the heat. Simmer gently over low heat with the cover ajar for 10 to 15 minutes, or until the sweet potatoes are just tender but still firm.

3 Add the beans, hominy, tomatoes, corn, chilis, cumin, and oregano. Simmer gently for 20 to 25 minutes longer. Stir in the cilantro, and taste first before adding salt (you may not need much, due to the canned beans and hominy). If desired, season with red pepper flakes if not using chipotle chilis.

4 The chili should have the consistency of a thick stew. Add a bit more water if too dense, but let it stay nice and thick. Serve at once, or let stand off the heat for an hour or so. Reheat before serving.

NOTE Chipotle chilis will give this chili a smokier, spicier flavor than either hot or mild green chilis are used.

POTAGE POLENTA WITH RED BEANS

A cornmeal porridge base with fresh and dried tomatoes　　6 to 8 servings

---

Cooked cornmeal makes a delightfully thick soup base. Accompany this meal-in-a-bowl with a colorful salad.

2 tablespoons olive oil

3 to 4 cloves garlic, minced

6 cups water

1 cup yellow cornmeal,
　　preferably stone ground

15-ounce can small red beans,
　　drained and rinsed

1 medium zucchini, quartered
　　lengthwise and sliced

1 cup diced ripe tomatoes

½ cup sun-dried tomatoes, oil-cured or
　　not, sliced (reserve half for topping)

1 teaspoon Italian seasoning

6 to 8 ounces chard (any variety) or kale,
　　well washed, stemmed, and chopped

Salt and freshly ground pepper to taste

A handful of basil leaves, cut into strips

1 cup mozzarella-style vegan cheese
　　shreds for topping, or as desired

1　Heat the oil in a soup pot. Add the garlic and sauté over low heat until golden.

2　Add 4 cups of the water and bring to a gentle simmer. Pour the cornmeal into the pot in a steady stream, ¼ cup at a time, whisking constantly.

3　Stir in the beans, fresh and dried tomatoes, and seasoning. Continue to simmer over low heat with the cover ajar. Uncover to whisk well every 5 minutes or so, for 25 minutes, or until the cornmeal is cooked. Whisk in 1 cup of water with each of the last two stirs.

4　Stir in the chard. Cook for 7 to 10 minutes, or until tender, but still bright green. Adjust the consistency with more water, if needed, but let the soup remain fairly thick.

5　Season with salt and pepper and serve. Garnish each serving with a few strips of basil, a sprinkling of cheese, and a few strips of the reserved sun-dried tomatoes.

FOUR GRAIN TOMATO SOUP

A medley of whole grains and vegetables in a tomato base
8 or more servings

This soup is fantastic served with Bruschetta (page 25) and your favorite prepared or home-made hummus or vegan pesto. It's also a great way to use up small amounts of whole grains you may have on hand, other than those listed below. Feel free to swap them in!

2 tablespoons olive oil
2 medium onions, quartered
   and thinly sliced
2 large celery stalks, finely diced
2 medium carrots, peeled and finely diced
2 medium potatoes (any variety),
   scrubbed and diced
28-ounce can crushed tomatoes
¼ cup raw brown rice, any variety
   (try basmati), rinsed
¼ cup raw wild rice, rinsed
¼ cup raw millet, rinsed
¼ cup raw pearl barley, rinsed
2 teaspoons salt-free seasoning
   (see page 8 for brands)
6 cups water
¼ cup chopped fresh dill
Salt and freshly ground pepper to taste

1 Heat the oil in a soup pot. Add the onions and sauté over medium-low heat until golden.

2 Add all the remaining ingredients except the dill, salt, and pepper. Bring to a slow boil, then lower the heat. Simmer gently over low heat with the cover ajar for 45 minutes to an hour, stirring every 15 minutes or so, or until the grains and vegetables are completely tender.

3 The soup should have a medium-thick consistency; not quite stew-like. If it's too thick, adjust the consistency with more water, as needed, and return to a gentle simmer.

4 Stir in the dill and season with salt and pepper. Serve at once, or if time allows, let the soup stand off the heat for an hour or two, then reheat before serving. This soup thickens quite a bit as it stands. Add water and adjust the seasonings as needed.

SPRING

After the thick, hearty soups of winter, spring soups give the palate a lift with lighter textures and flavors. They set the stage for a meal, taking the edge off of hunger yet leave plenty of room for other courses and accompaniments.

SPRING VEGETABLE SOUP

Potatoes, carrots, and peas in a light broth

This light soup, with its mildly seasoned broth, is festive enough to serve as a first course of a spring holiday meal—and so easy to prepare that it can also be enjoyed as everyday fare.

1 tablespoon olive oil

1 large or 2 medium leeks, white
    parts only, quartered lengthwise,
    chopped, and well rinsed

2 medium celery stalks, diced

32-ounce carton vegetable broth
    plus 2 cups water or 6 cups water
    with 2 vegetable bouillon cubes

3 medium potatoes, peeled and diced

3 medium carrots, peeled and thinly sliced

1 medium red or yellow bell
    pepper, or half of each

2 teaspoons salt-free seasoning
    (see page 8 for brands)

1 ½ cups finely chopped tomatoes

1 ½ cups shelled fresh or frozen green peas

¼ cup chopped fresh parsley or a big
    handful of baby spinach, sliced

1 to 2 tablespoons minced
    fresh dill, optional

Salt and freshly ground pepper to taste

1 Heat the oil in a soup pot. Add the leeks and celery and sauté over medium-low heat until the leeks are limp, stirring occasionally, about 8 minutes.

2 Add the broth and water, potatoes, carrots, bell pepper, and seasoning. Bring to a slow boil, then lower the heat. Simmer gently over low heat with the cover ajar for 15 to 20 minutes, or until the vegetables are tender.

3 Stir in the tomatoes, peas, parsley, and optional dill. Cook over very low heat for 6 to 7 minutes longer. Make sure the peas and parsley stay nice and green (or see Note if making ahead of time). If the soup is crowded, add another cup or so of water and heat through.

4 Season with salt and pepper and serve at once.

NOTE If you're making this soup ahead of time, hold off on adding the peas and parsley (or spinach), and optional dill. Once the soup is reheated and ready to be served, add these last ingredients.

LEMONY SPINACH ORZO SOUP

With leeks, bell pepper, and tiny pasta

6 to 8 servings

Here's a lively soup that comes together quickly. For a light, satisfying meal, serve with a big Greek-style salad — with a generous sprinkling of vegan feta on top.

**2 medium leeks, white and
    palest green parts**
1 ½ tablespoons olive oil
1 medium red bell pepper, diced
2 to 3 cloves garlic, minced
6 cups water
2 vegetable bouillon cubes
**14.5-ounce can diced tomatoes
    (try fire roasted)**
¾ cup orzo (rice-shaped pasta)
5 ounces baby spinach
**¼ cup chopped fresh parsley,
    or more, to taste**
¼ cup chopped fresh dill
Zest and juice of 1 lemon, or more, to taste
Salt and freshly ground pepper to taste
Lemon slices for garnish, optional

1 Trim away the ends and dark green leaves of the leeks and discard. Cut the leeks in half lengthwise, then into ¼-inch half-rings. Place in a colander and rinse very well, making sure that any grit is washed away.

2 Heat the oil in a soup pot. Add the leeks and sauté over medium-low heat until limp. Add the bell pepper and garlic and continue to sauté until the leeks are golden.

3 Add the water, bouillon cubes, and tomatoes. Bring to a slow boil, then lower the heat. Simmer gently over low heat with the cover ajar for 10 minutes.

4 Meanwhile, cook the orzo in a separate saucepan until *al dente*, then drain. Add the cooked orzo to the soup, along with the spinach and herbs.

5 Stir in the lemon zest and juice. If the soup is too dense, add a small amount of water. Season with salt and pepper.

6 Serve at once. Garnish each bowlful with a couple of lemon slices, if you'd like.

SPINACH CHICKPEA NOODLE SOUP

A warming melange of flavor, texture, and color   6 servings

With an extra yum factor from the wide noodles, this mildly spiced soup can be made with baby arugula, watercress, or other tender greens in place of spinach.

1 ½ tablespoons olive oil
1 medium onion, finely chopped
3 medium carrots, peeled and thinly sliced
2 large stalks celery, diced
2 cloves garlic, minced
6 cups water
2 vegetable bouillon cubes
14.5-ounce can diced tomatoes
15-ounce can chickpeas, drained and rinsed
2 teaspoons good-quality curry powder
Pinch each: ground nutmeg
    and coriander, optional
6 ounces (about half of a 12-ounce
    package) egg-free ribbon noodles
    (see options in Note)
5 ounces baby spinach
¼ cup chopped fresh cilantro, optional
Salt and freshly ground pepper to taste

1   Heat the oil in a large soup pot. Add the onion, carrots, celery, and garlic. Sauté over medium-low heat until all are golden.

2   Add the water, bouillon cubes, tomatoes, chickpeas, curry powder, and optional spices. Bring to a slow boil, then lower the heat. Simmer gently over low heat with the cover ajar for 15 to 20 minutes.

3   Cook the noodles in a separate pot according to package directions until *al dente*, then drain.

4   Stir the noodles, spinach, and optional cilantro into the soup pot. Cook for a minute or two, just until the spinach is wilted. Season with salt and pepper. Add a bit more water if the broth is crowded.

5   The noodles will absorb the broth as the soup stands. Add more water and adjust the seasonings as needed.

NOTE Other noodles that can be used in this soup, if you can't find egg-free ribbons: thin spaghetti (broken into short pieces), ditalini, tiny shells, or rombi.

CREOLE POTAGE MAIGRE

A classic soup featuring lettuce, cucumber, and peas

6 to 8 servings

This light soup of lettuce, cucumber, and fresh spring peas was quite common in 19th-century American cuisine. Potage maigre translates loosely as "lean" or "meager" soup, referring to the absence of meat. That's why it was traditionally served for Lent and other fast days. Versions of it appear in old Creole cookbooks.

2 tablespoons olive oil

2 large onions, quartered and thinly sliced

1 large celery stalk, finely diced

Handful of celery leaves

2 small heads Boston or Bibb
   lettuce, finely shredded

32-ounce carton vegetable broth
   plus 1 cup water, or 5 cups water
   with 2 vegetable bouillon cubes

1 cup steamed fresh or thawed
   frozen green peas

1 cup peeled, seeded cucumber, grated

¼ cup chopped fresh parsley

2 tablespoons chopped fresh dill,
   or more to taste

Salt and freshly ground pepper to taste

Vegan sour cream (homemade, page 7,
   or from an 8-ounce tub), optional

1   Heat the oil in a soup pot. Add the onions and sauté over medium-low heat until translucent. Add the celery and continue to sauté until both are golden.

2   Add the celery leaves, lettuce, and broth. Bring to a slow boil, then lower the heat. Simmer gently over low heat with the cover ajar for 10 minutes, or until the lettuce is wilted but still has a bit of crunch.

3   Add the peas and cucumber. Adjust the consistency with additional water if the soup is crowded. Stir in the parsley and dill, then season with salt and lots of freshly ground pepper. Simmer over low heat for 5 minutes longer.

4   Serve at once. Top each serving with a dollop of sour cream, if desired.

ASPARAGUS & SPINACH SOUP

With wild rice and mushrooms

6 servings

An earthy medley of colors, textures, and flavors, you'll love serving this soup on rainy spring evenings.

1 ¼ cups water
½ cup raw wild rice, rinsed
10 to 12 ounces asparagus
6 ounces fresh shiitake mushrooms,
 stemmed and sliced
1 large carrot, peeled and coarsely grated
 (or about a cup of pre-grated carrot)
1 medium yellow summer squash, diced
4 to 5 scallions, sliced
32-ounce carton vegetable broth or 4 cups
 water with 2 vegetable bouillon cubes
1 ½ teaspoons salt-free seasoning
 (see page 8 for brands)
¼ cup dry white wine, optional
5 ounces baby spinach
2 tablespoons chopped fresh dill,
 or more, to taste
Salt and freshly ground pepper to taste

1 Bring the water to a boil in a small saucepan. Add the wild rice, then lower the heat and simmer gently with the cover ajar until the water is absorbed, about 35 minutes.

2 Meanwhile, trim about 1 inch from the ends of the asparagus, and peel the bottom halves of the stalks with a vegetable peeler. Cut into 1-inch pieces.

3 Combine the asparagus with the remaining ingredients (except the spinach, dill, salt, and pepper) in a soup pot. There should be enough liquid to just cover the vegetables; add water as needed. Bring to a slow boil, then lower the heat. Simmer gently over low heat with the cover ajar for about 15 minutes, or until the vegetables are just tender. Remove from the heat.

4 When the wild rice is done, stir it into the soup, followed by the spinach and dill. Cover and cook until the spinach has wilted, then season with salt and pepper. Adjust the consistency with enough additional water (1 to 2 cups) to give the soup a slightly dense consistency.

5 Continue to cook for 2 to 3 minutes, just until piping hot, then serve.

PUREE OF ASPARAGUS WITH SOBA

Garnished with toasted almonds   6 servings

Nutty-tasting Japanese soba (buckwheat noodles) add an offbeat touch to this soup. Look for them in natural foods stores and Asian groceries.

2 pounds asparagus

1 tablespoon dark sesame oil

1 large onion, chopped

32-ounce carton vegetable broth or 4 cups water with 2 vegetable bouillon cubes

2 large celery stalks, diced

2 medium potatoes, scrubbed and diced

2 tablespoons soy sauce or tamari, or to taste

4 ounces soba (buckwheat noodles)

Freshly ground pepper to taste

½ cup slivered or sliced toasted almonds, for garnish

Sliced scallions or minced chives for garnish

1 Trim the woody ends from the asparagus, peel the bottom halves with a vegetable peeler, and cut into 1-inch lengths. Reserve and set aside the tips.

2 Heat the oil in a large soup pot. Add the onion and sauté over medium-low heat until golden. Add the broth, celery, potatoes, and soy sauce. Bring to a slow boil, then lower the heat. Simmer gently over low heat with the cover ajar for 10 minutes.

3 Add the asparagus pieces (except the reserved tips) and simmer for 15 minutes longer, or until the vegetables are tender. Remove from the heat.

4 With a slotted spoon, transfer the solid ingredients to a food processor or blender with a little of the liquid. Puree in batches until smooth and stir back into the soup pot. Or, skip the food processor and insert an immersion blender into the pot and blend the soup until pureed to your liking. Let the soup stand off the heat, covered.

5 Break the soba noodles into 2-inch lengths. In a separate saucepan, cook them in rapidly simmering water until *al dente*. Drain them, then stir them into the soup.

6 In the same saucepan, steam the reserved asparagus tips until bright green and tender-crisp, then stir into the soup.

7 Adjust the consistency of the soup with enough water to give it a slightly thick consistency. Season with freshly ground pepper and more soy sauce, if needed. Serve at once. Garnish each serving with a sprinkling of almonds and scallions.

SPICY ASPARAGUS & GREEN BEAN STEW

With red bell peppers and baked tofu

I enjoy the tender green beans of late spring, though I do find them to be a temperamental vegetable—you never know just how long they'll take to cook. That's why I recommend steaming the green beans separately, and adding them to the soup once the asparagus is tender-crisp.

1 pound fresh green beans,
   trimmed and cut in half
1 tablespoon dark sesame oil
1 medium onion, finely chopped
4 to 5 cloves garlic, minced
2 cups water
1 pound slender asparagus, woody ends
   trimmed, cut into 1 ½-inch lengths
2 medium red bell peppers, cut
   into short narrow strips
2 to 3 teaspoons grated fresh or
   bottled ginger, to taste
8-ounce package baked tofu, any
   variety, cut into ½-inch dice
1 to 2 teaspoons sriracha or other
   hot sauce, or to taste
2 to 3 tablespoons soy sauce
   or tamari, or to taste
2 tablespoons cornstarch
Hot cooked rice or noodles, optional

1 In a large saucepan, steam the green beans in an inch or so of water, covered, until tender-crisp. Stir occasionally. When done, remove from the heat and rinse briefly with cool water.

2 Meanwhile, heat the oil in a soup pot. Add the onion and garlic and sauté over medium heat, stirring frequently, until the onion is lightly golden.

3 Add the water, asparagus, bell peppers, and ginger. Bring to a slow boil, then lower the heat. Simmer gently over low heat with the cover ajar for 10 minutes, or until the asparagus and bell pepper are tender-crisp.

4 Add the tofu, sriracha, soy sauce, and steamed green beans. Stir together and return the mixture to a gentle simmer.

5 Dissolve the cornstarch in a small amount of water. Stir slowly into the stew. Simmer over very low heat, uncovered, for 5 minutes longer.

6 Serve the stew at once, on its own or over hot cooked rice or noodles.

FESTIVE BEET BORSCHT

A gorgeous Eastern European soup
6 to 8 servings

Filled with year-round produce, borscht is as good (maybe better) served chilled as it is hot. If it weren't for the fact that it's a bit messy to make, I'd put this one on the rotation more regularly! I most enjoy alternating it throughout Passover week in the spring (after we've had our fill of vegan matzo ball soup). It's also a classic choice for Rosh Hashanah (the Jewish New Year) in the early fall.

6 medium beets, peeled and cut
    into large chunks (see Note)
4 medium carrots, peeled and
    cut into large chunks
1 large sweet apple, peeled,
    cored, and cut into chunks
1 large onion, cut into chunks
Juice of 1 to 2 lemons, (¼ to ½
    cup) or more, to taste
¼ cup natural granulated sugar
    or agave, or more, to taste
Pinch of salt
Freshly ground pepper to taste
¼ cup minced fresh dill, plus more
    for garnish
Vegan sour cream (homemade,
    page 7, or an 8-ounce tub)

1 Grate the beets, carrots, apple, and onion in a food processor fitted with the grating blade. As the work bowl gets filled, transfer the grated ingredients to a large soup pot.

2 Add enough water to cover the grated ingredients, then add the lemon juice, sugar, and salt. Bring to a slow boil, then lower the heat. Simmer gently over low heat with the cover ajar until everything is tender, about 20 to 30 minutes.

3 Adjust the consistency with more water if the vegetables are crowded. Add the salt (or, you can skip it if you'd like; this is the rare savory soup that doesn't need it) and season with pepper. Taste and add more lemon juice and/or sugar to adjust the sweet and tangy balance to your liking.

4 This is a good soup to make ahead of time. If you'd like to serve it chilled (which is how it shines), let it cool to room temperature, then refrigerate, covered, until chilled. To serve hot, simply serve as soon as the soup is done, or reheat before serving.

5 Just before serving, stir in the dill. Top each serving with a dollop of sour cream and more fresh dill.

NOTE Peeling raw beets is no fun. Make it a bit easier by microwaving them briefly in a covered container (allowing 2 minutes per beet), then plunge them into cold water for a bit. Peeling will be easier, and the beets will cook more quickly, too.

CREAMY PARSLEY POTATO SOUP

With a luscious vegan cream cheese base

6 to 8 servings

Lots of fresh parsley and vegan cream cheese give this soup its special savor.

1 tablespoon olive oil

1 large onion, chopped

2 cloves garlic, minced

32-ounce container vegetable
   broth or 4 cups water with 2
   vegetable bouillon cubes

6 medium potatoes (any variety),
   peeled and diced

2 teaspoons all-purpose seasoning blend

4 ounces vegan cream cheese
   (from an 8-ounce tub)

½ cup chopped fresh parsley

2 to 4 tablespoons minced
   fresh dill, to taste

¼ cup quick-cooking oats (oatmeal)

2 cups unsweetened plant-
   based milk, or as needed

Salt and freshly ground pepper to taste

1   Heat the oil in a soup pot. Add the onion and sauté over medium-low heat until translucent. Add the garlic and continue to sauté until both are golden.

2   Add the broth, potatoes, and seasoning. Bring to a slow boil, then lower the heat. Simmer gently over low heat with the cover ajar until the potatoes are tender, about 20 minutes.

3   Remove about ½ cup of the hot liquid with a ladle and transfer it to a small mixing bowl. Combine with the cream cheese and whisk together until smooth. Stir into the soup along with the parsley and dill.

4   Slowly sprinkle in the oats. Simmer for 20 to 25 minutes over very low heat, or until the potatoes are completely tender.

5   Add enough plant-based milk to give the soup a slightly thick consistency, then season with salt and pepper. Heat through and serve. This soup thickens as it stands. Add more plant-based milk as needed, then adjust the seasonings.

PUREE OF SPRING GREENS

An intense blend of tender greens and parsley

When you have a surplus of greens from the farmers market or your CSA share, this puree of leafy greens soup helps use them up deliciously.

2 tablespoons olive oil

1 large onion, chopped

2 to 3 cloves garlic, minced

32-ounce carton vegetable broth or 4 cups
    water with 2 vegetable bouillon cubes

2 large or 3 medium potatoes,
    peeled and diced

2 pounds or so leafy greens (choose
    any 3 or 4 listed in Note)

½ to 1 cup parsley leaves

1 to 2 cups unsweetened plant-based
    milk, or as needed

Salt and freshly ground pepper to taste

Vegan sour cream (homemade, page 7,
    or from an 8-ounce tub), optional

1 Heat the oil in a soup pot. Add the onion and sauté over medium-low heat until translucent. Add the garlic and continue to sauté until both are golden.

2 Add broth and potatoes. Bring to a slow boil, then lower the heat. Simmer gently over low heat with the cover ajar until the potatoes are tender, about 15 to 20 minutes.

3 Make sure your greens of choice are well washed. Remove any thick midribs and chop leaves coarsely.

4 Once the potatoes are tender, add any hardy greens (like kale or collards) you're using and cover. Simmer gently for 5 to 7 minutes, or until nearly tender and still bright green,

5 Add any tender greens you're using, along with the parsley. Cook until the tender greens are wilted.

6 Puree the mixture (in batches if need be) in a blender until smooth. Return to the soup pot and stir in enough plant-based milk to give the soup a slightly thick consistency. Or, skip the food processor and insert an immersion blender into the pot and blend the soup until pureed to your liking.

7 Season with salt and pepper and serve. Pass around sour cream for garnish if you'd like.

NOTE Choose from among 3 or 4 of the following, or any other leafy greens you have on hand: arugula; Asian greens (baby bok choy, tatsoi, mizuna); chard (any variety); collard greens; escarole; green lettuce (any variety); kale; spinach.

POTATO DILL SOUP WITH GREEN BEANS

A warming soup with the fresh taste of dill

The fresh flavor of dill makes this simple soup a good choice for the transitional period between winter and spring. It's perfect for those inevitable chilly, rainy spring evenings.

1 tablespoon olive oil

1 medium onion, finely chopped

2 to 3 cloves garlic, minced

4 to 5 medium golden potatoes, scrubbed and diced

28-ounce can diced tomatoes (Italian or fire roasted)

¼ cup dry white or red wine, optional

1 teaspoon ground cumin

1 teaspoon paprika

2 teaspoons salt-free seasoning (see page 8 for brands)

15-ounce can pink beans, drained and rinsed

2 cups frozen cut green beans, thawed

¼ cup chopped fresh dill, or more, to taste

¼ cup chopped fresh parsley

Salt and freshly ground pepper to taste

1 Heat the oil in a soup pot. Add the onion and sauté over medium-low heat until translucent. Add the garlic and continue to sauté until both are golden.

2 Add the potatoes with just enough water to cover, followed by the tomatoes, optional wine, and spices. Bring to a slow boil, then lower the heat. Simmer gently over low heat with the cover ajar for 20 minutes.

3 Stir in the pink beans, green beans, and enough additional water to give the soup a slightly dense consistency (about 2 cups). Continue to simmer for 15 minutes longer, or until the vegetables are tender, but not overdone.

4 Stir in the dill and parsley, then season with salt and pepper. Serve at once, or if time allows, let the soup stand off the heat for an hour or two, then heat through before serving.

CREAM OF CAULIFLOWER SOUP

A mild puree with a flourish of colorful vegetables 6 servings

This creamy soup, enhanced with any of the garnishes recommended, makes a hearty, but not heavy, first course. It can even star as the centerpiece of a spring meal.

1 tablespoon olive oil
1 cup chopped onion
2 to 4 cloves garlic, minced
32-ounce carton vegetable broth or 4 cups
    water with 2 vegetable bouillon cubes
1 large head cauliflower, chopped
    into 2-inch chunks
2 medium potatoes (any variety),
    peeled and diced
2 teaspoons salt-free seasoning
    (see page 8 for brands)
1 teaspoon ground cumin
14.5-ounce can Great Northern beans
    or cannellini, drained and rinsed
1 ½ to 2 cups unsweetened plant-
    based milk, or as needed
Salt and freshly ground pepper to taste

Garnishes (choose any 2 or 3 of these)
Steamed finely chopped broccoli
    florets (about 1 cup)
Steamed chopped spinach (about 1 cup)
Steamed fresh green peas (about ¾ cup)
Steamed red bell pepper strips
    (from about 1 medium pepper)
Chopped fresh herbs (about ½ cup);
    try any combination of parsley,
    dill, chives, and oregano

1 Heat the oil in a soup pot. Add the onion and sauté over medium-low heat until translucent. Add the garlic and continue to sauté until both are golden.

2 Add the broth, cauliflower, potatoes, salt-free seasoning, and cumin. Bring to a slow boil, then lower the heat. Simmer gently over low heat with the cover ajar for about 20 minutes, or until the vegetables are tender. Remove from the heat.

3 Use a slotted spoon to transfer the vegetables to a food processor or blender and puree, in batches if necessary, until smooth. Puree about half of the beans with each batch of vegetables. Transfer the puree back to the soup pot and stir it back into any remaining liquid. Or, add all the beans to the soup pot, insert an immersion blender, and process until pureed to your liking.

4 Stir in enough plant-based milk to give the soup a medium-thick consistency. Season with salt and pepper. If time allows, let the soup stand off the heat for 1 to 2 hours then reheat before serving. Top each serving with 2 or 3 of the garnishes.

CURRIED CAULIFLOWER CHEESE SOUP

A chunky, mildly spiced soup with peas and cilantro   6 to 8 servings

---

*If you're looking for a mild, soothing soup for a
rainy spring evening, here's a pleasing choice.*

2 tablespoons olive oil

1 large onion, chopped

2 medium celery stalks, diced

32-ounce carton vegetable broth or 4 cups
    water with 2 vegetable bouillon cubes

3 medium potatoes (any variety),
    peeled and diced

1 medium head cauliflower, finely chopped

2 teaspoons good-quality curry
    powder, more or less to taste

1 ½ to 2 cups unsweetened plant-
    based milk, or as needed

1 cup steamed fresh or thawed
    frozen green peas

¼ to ½ cup fresh cilantro, to taste

1 cup firmly packed mozzarella or
    jack-style vegan cheese shreds

Salt and freshly ground pepper to taste

1 Heat the oil in a soup pot. Add the onion and
celery and sauté over medium-low heat until both
are golden.

2 Add the broth, potatoes, cauliflower, and curry
powder. Bring to a slow boil, then lower the heat.
Simmer gently over low heat with the cover ajar for
about 20 to 25 minutes, or until all the vegetables are
tender. Remove from the heat.

3 Using a slotted spoon, transfer half of the solid
ingredients to a food processor or blender. Process
until smoothly pureed. Stir back into the remaining
soup. Or, insert an immersion blender into the soup
and process until about half of the ingredients are
pureed.

4 Add just enough plant-based milk to give the
soup a slightly thick consistency. Stir in the peas and
cilantro, then return to low heat and bring to a gentle
simmer.

5 Sprinkle in the cheese a little at a time, stirring
until fairly well melted each time. Season to taste
with salt and pepper. Simmer gently for 2 to 3 minutes longer, then serve.

 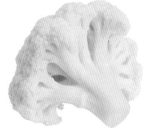 

EASY LAKSA SOUP

A vegan twist on a Southeast Asian classic

Vegan laksa soup is made easily courtesy of some good-quality shortcuts. A dish of Southeast Asian origins (Malaysia, Singapore, and Indonesia), it features rice noodles in a coconut-curry broth with vegetables and tasty toppings.

4-ounce bundle flat rice noodles or linguine

1 tablespoon neutral vegetable oil

1 medium onion, finely chopped

4 to 5 cloves garlic, minced

32-ounce carton vegetable broth or 4 cups
  water with 2 vegetable bouillon cubes

12-ounce jar Indian simmer sauce,
  any dairy-free variety (see Note)

2 to 3 teaspoons grated fresh
  or bottled ginger

Juice of 1 lime

1 teaspoon good-quality curry powder

15-ounce can chickpeas, drained and rinsed

2 to 3 big handfuls baby spinach or 2 cups
  finely chopped broccoli florets

¼ cup cilantro leaves

13.5-ounce can light coconut milk

Salt and freshly ground pepper to taste

Dried hot red pepper flakes
  or sriracha to taste

For topping (use any or all)

Mung bean sprouts or green sprouts

More cilantro leaves

½ medium red bell pepsper, finely diced

Sesame seeds

1 Cook the noodles according to package directions until *al dente*, then drain and cut into shorter lengths.

2 Meanwhile, heat the oil in a soup pot. Add the onion and sauté over medium-low heat until translucent. Add the garlic and continue to sauté until both are golden.

3 Add the broth, simmer sauce, ginger, lime juice, curry powder, and chickpeas (reserve a few for topping, if you'd like). Bring to a slow boil, then lower the heat. Simmer gently over low heat with the cover ajar for 5 minutes.

4 Stir in the broccoli and simmer briefly, just until bright green. Stir in the cilantro and coconut milk.

5 Simmer for another minute or so until heated through, then season with salt, pepper, and hot seasoning (or pass it around for individual servings).

6 Serve at once. Top each serving with your choice of toppings, as well as any reserved chickpeas. The soup thickens quite a bit as it stands; adjust with water as needed.

NOTE Indian simmer sauces are available in the Asian foods section of well-stocked supermarkets. Dairy-free choices include Madras curry (which is fairly spicy), Goan coconut, rogan josh, and jalfrezi.

VEGETABLE VARIATIONS In place of broccoli or spinach, try swapping in cauliflower, green peas, or green beans.

CURRIED CASHEW VEGETABLE SOUP

With notes of ginger, curry, and citrus   6 to 8 servings

Pureed cashews make an irresistibly rich-tasting soup base. This luscious soup is a good way to use up bits of green vegetables that may be lingering in your refrigerator or freezer.

1 heaping cup unsalted toasted cashews
1 ½ tablespoons olive oil
2 large onions, chopped
3 to 4 cloves garlic, minced
1 large celery stalk, diced
3 cups water
2 teaspoons minced fresh or
    bottled ginger, or to taste
2 teaspoons good-quality curry
    powder, or to taste
1 teaspoon ground cumin
Pinch of nutmeg
1 tablespoon lemon juice, or more, to taste
½ cup orange juice, preferably fresh
3 cups steamed fresh or frozen green
    vegetables (such as finely chopped
    broccoli, green peas, diced zucchini,
    cut green beans, or any combination)
Salt and freshly ground pepper to taste
Thinly sliced scallions for garnish
Chopped cashews for garnish, optional

1   In a heatproof bowl, combine the cashews with enough boiling water to cover. Let stand for at least 30 minutes.

2   Heat the oil in a soup pot. Add the onions, garlic, and celery and sauté over medium-low heat until all are lightly browned.

3   Transfer the onion mixture to a food processor or blender with the soaked cashews and their water. Process until smoothly pureed (add a small amount of water, if more is needed, to get things moving), then transfer back to the soup pot.

4   Add the 3 cups of water and bring to a simmer. Stir in the ginger, curry powder, cumin, nutmeg, lemon juice, and orange juice. Bring to a slow boil, then lower the heat. Simmer gently over low heat with the cover ajar for 15 minutes.

5   Stir in the steamed vegetables. If the soup is too dense, add enough water to give it a slightly thick consistency.

6   Season with salt and pepper, then serve. Garnish each serving with a sprinkling of scallions and, if desired, a few chopped cashews.

MASALA VEGETABLE STEW

A medley of mixed vegetables in coconut broth   6 to 8 servings

This hearty stew becomes the centerpiece of a satisfying meal, either served on its own or over hot cooked grains. Add fresh flatbread and a palate-cooling salad of cucumbers and tomatoes dressed in coconut yogurt. This aromatic stew features Indian simmer sauce, one of my favorite shortcuts to flavor.

2 tablespoons olive oil

1 medium onion, chopped

2 to 3 cloves garlic, minced

2 cups baby carrots (thick ones
   halved lengthwise)

2 cups water

1 medium eggplant, stemmed and diced

2 medium potatoes (any variety),
   scrubbed and diced

1 large green or red bell pepper, diced

14.5-ounce can diced tomatoes

1 to 2 teaspoons grated fresh or
   bottled ginger, to taste

1 to 2 fresh hot chili peppers,
   seeded and minced, optional

12-ounce jar Indian simmer sauce (see Note)

13.5-ounce can light coconut milk

1 cup frozen green peas, thawed

¼ cup chopped fresh cilantro, optional

Salt to taste

Hot cooked basmati rice or
   couscous, optional

1 Heat the oil in a soup pot and add the onion, garlic, and carrots. Sauté over medium-low heat until all are golden.

2 Add the water, eggplant, potatoes, bell pepper, tomatoes, ginger, and chili peppers. Bring to a slow boil, then lower the heat. Simmer gently over low heat with the cover ajar for 20 to 25 minutes, or until the vegetables are just tender.

3 Stir in the simmer sauce, coconut milk, peas, and cilantro. Return to a gentle simmer. Simmer over low heat, uncovered, for an additional 5 to 10 minutes longer.

4 Serve the stew on its own, or ladled over hot cooked rice or couscous.

NOTE Indian simmer sauces are available in the Asian foods section of well-stocked supermarkets. Dairy-free varieties include Madras curry (which is fairly spicy), Goan coconut, rogan josh, and jalfrezi.

VARIATIONS Feel free to substitute other vegetables for those listed. Instead of eggplant, substitute a medium head of cauliflower, chopped into bite-size pieces; or use corn kernels in place of the peas. Sweet potato can be swapped in for regular potatoes.

COUNTRY CAPTAIN STEW

A mildly curried vegetable mélange with apples and tofu 6 servings

Although it bears a passing resemblance to the classic East Indian mulligatawny soup), this recipe is actually an adaptation of a classic curried chicken stew from the American South. This veganized version swaps in baked tofu. The harmony of sweet and savory flavors in a curried base is most appealing.

2 tablespoons olive oil

1 large or 2 medium onions, chopped

3 to 4 cloves garlic, minced

2 cups water

1 large green bell pepper, cut into strips

4 medium golden potatoes, scrubbed
   and cut into ½-inch dice

14.5-ounce can diced tomatoes

2 Granny Smith apples, peeled,
   cored, and diced

2 teaspoons good quality curry
   powder, or to taste

1 to 2 teaspoons grated fresh or
   bottled ginger, to taste

Pinch of cayenne pepper or dried
   hot red pepper flakes

8-ounce package baked tofu,
   cut into small dice

½ cup dark raisins

½ cup finely chopped fresh
   cilantro or parsley

Salt and freshly ground pepper to taste

Vegan yogurt for topping, optional
   (coconut yogurt works well)

1 Heat the oil in a soup pot. Add the onion and sauté over medium heat until translucent. Add the garlic and continue to sauté until both are golden.

2 Add the water, bell pepper, potatoes, tomatoes, apples, curry powder, ginger, and cayenne pepper. Bring to a slow boil, then lower the heat. Simmer gently over low heat with the cover ajar for about 20 minutes, or until the potatoes are done.

3 Stir in the baked tofu, raisins, and cilantro. Add a little more water, if needed, but let the stew remain thick. Season with salt and pepper.

4 Cook over very low heat for 10 to 15 minutes. Serve at once or make ahead and reheat when needed. Top each serving with a dollop of vegan yogurt, if desired.

SPANISH VEGETABLE STEW

Wine-scented vegetables and artichokes   6 servings

Menestra de verduras, *a classic Spanish dish, has many regional variations and can be made with different vegetables according to season. It's not often vegan, but this recipe shows how easy it is to make it plant-base. Characteristic ingredients include potatoes, carrots, and green peas, and artichokes. Fresh artichokes are called for in traditional recipes, but using the canned variety simplifies the process immensely. The wine gives off a wonderful aroma as the stew cooks.*

2 tablespoons extra-virgin olive oil

1 large onion, quartered and thinly sliced

2 to 3 cloves garlic, minced

3 cups vegetable broth or water
   with 1 vegetable bouillon cube

½ cup dry white wine

3 large potatoes, peeled and diced

3 medium carrots, peeled and sliced

8 ounces white or cremini mushrooms,
   stemmed and sliced

1 ½ teaspoons sweet or Spanish paprika

½ teaspoon ground cumin

12 stalks asparagus, bottoms trimmed,
   and cut into 1-inch pieces

15-ounce can artichoke hearts,
   drained and quartered

1 cup frozen green peas, thawed

½ cup chopped fresh parsley or cilantro

Juice of ½ to 1 lemon, to taste

Salt and freshly ground pepper to taste

1   Heat the oil in a soup pot. Add the onion and sauté over medium-low heat until translucent. Add the garlic and continue to sauté until both are golden.

2   Add the broth, wine, potatoes, carrots, mushrooms, paprika, and cumin. Bring to a slow boil, then lower the heat. Simmer gently over low heat with the cover ajar for 15 to 20 minutes, or until the potatoes and carrots are tender.

3   Add the asparagus and cook over low heat until it is tender, but still bright green, about 10 minutes.

4   Stir in the artichoke hearts, peas, and parsley. Season with lemon juice, salt, and pepper. Cook over low heat for 5 minutes longer.

5   If the stew is too dense, add a bit more broth, then adjust the seasonings. Serve at once.

ASPARAGUS ARBORIO RICE SOUP

Mushroom and asparagus risotto transformed into a thick soup   6 servings

---

Arborio rice, an Italian variety that gives risotto its creamy texture, makes a cozy base for this spring soup.

1 tablespoon olive oil

1 medium onion, finely chopped

2 to 3 cloves garlic, minced

32-ounce carton vegetable broth

4 cups water

¾ cups raw arborio rice

8 to 10 ounces cremini mushrooms, cleaned, stemmed, and sliced

1 teaspoon dried basil

12 asparagus stalks, bottoms trimmed, and cut into ½-inch lengths

1 cup fresh or thawed frozen green peas

1 cup diced fresh tomatoes

¼ to ½ cup minced fresh parsley

½ cup sliced sun-dried tomatoes (oil-cured or not, as desired)

Salt and freshly ground pepper to taste

1 Heat the oil in a soup pot. Add the onion and sauté over medium-low heat until translucent. Add the garlic and continue to sauté until both are golden.

2 Add the broth, 2 cups of the water, rice, mushrooms, and basil. Bring to a slow boil, then lower the heat. Simmer gently over low heat with the cover ajar for 15 to 20 minutes, stirring occasionally, or until the rice is tender.

3 Stir in the asparagus and the remaining 2 cups water. Cover and cook for 5 minutes longer.

4 Add the peas, tomatoes, parsley, and dried tomatoes. Heat through and add more water, as needed, to give the soup a thick but still soupy consistency. Season with salt and pepper and serve.

CREOLE EGGPLANT SOUP

A great way to feature eggplant in a thick soup 6 servings

Years ago, while traveling through New Orleans, this classic soup was one of my favorite discoveries. I enjoy make when the mood for eggplant strikes.

2 tablespoons olive oil
1 large onion, chopped
3 medium celery stalks, diced
1 clove garlic, minced
1 ½ tablespoons unbleached white flour
2 large or 4 medium potatoes,
    scrubbed and finely diced
1 large or 2 medium eggplants (1 ½ pounds
    total), stemmed and cut into ½-inch dice
Water, as needed
1 teaspoon dried basil
½ teaspoon dried thyme
1 ½ teaspoons good-quality curry
    powder, or more to taste
¼ cup chopped fresh parsley
1 ½ cups unsweetened plant-
    based milk, or as needed
Salt and freshly ground pepper to taste

1 Heat the oil in a large soup pot. Add the onion, celery, and garlic. Sauté over medium-low heat until all are golden. Sprinkle in the flour and stir for a minute or so.

2 Add the potatoes and eggplant, along with just enough water to barely cover the vegetables. Bring to a slow boil.

3 Lower the heat add the basil, thyme, and curry, and stir well. Simmer gently over low heat with the cover ajar for 25 minutes, or until the vegetables are tender.

4 Stir in the parsley and enough plant-based milk to give the soup a slightly thick consistency. Season with salt and pepper.

5 Simmer over very low heat for 5 to 10 minutes longer. Serve at once, or if time allows, let the soup stand off the heat for an hour or so, then reheat before serving.

OKRA RICE SOUP

A vegan cousin of Creole gumbo

A true Southern classic, okra rice soup was as commonplace in the 19th century as it is offbeat today. For this recipe, it's best to use young, tender okra, about 3 inches in length. The result is a wonderfully complex blend of flavors and textures. Any kind of fresh cornbread pairs wonderfully with this soup. Make Green Chili Cornbread (page 24) or Cheese and Herb Corn Muffins (page 21) while the soup is simmering.

1 ½ tablespoons olive oil

2 medium onions, quartered
   and thinly sliced

2 medium celery stalks, finely diced

6 cups water

6 medium or 4 large ripe, juicy tomatoes
   (about 1 ½ pounds), diced

3 to 3 ½ cups fresh young okra,
   stemmed and sliced ½ inch thick

1 medium green bell pepper, diced

⅔ cup raw long-grain white rice
   (jasmine rice works well)

2 teaspoons fresh thyme leaves,
   or 1 teaspoon dried

Dried hot red pepper flakes or
   cayenne pepper to taste

Salt and freshly ground pepper to taste

¼ cup chopped fresh parsley,
   or more to taste

1   Heat the oil in a large soup pot. Add the onions sauté until over medium-low heat until translucent. Add the celery and continue to sauté over low heat until both are golden.

2   Add the water, followed by all the remaining ingredients except the salt, pepper, and parsley. Use discretion with the hot seasoning (you can always add more later if you want a spicier soup, or pass it around at the table).

3   Bring to a slow boil, then lower the heat. Simmer gently over low heat with the cover ajar for about 25 minutes, until the rice is cooked and the vegetables are tender. Season with salt and pepper.

4   If time allows, let the soup stand for an hour or so, then heat through as needed. It will thicken considerably as it stands. Adjust the consistency with a more water, as needed, but let it remain thick.

5   Just before serving, stir in the parsley. Taste to adjust the seasonings, reheat, and serve.

THAI-FLAVORED VEGETABLE STEW

A medley of vegetables in coconut-peanut sauce   6 or more servings

In this Thai-inspired vegetable stew, broccoli, cauliflower, green beans, and peppers are enveloped in a rich coconut peanut sauce. Served over rice noodles, it's a delectable one-dish meal.

**4-ounce bundle thin Asian rice
 noodles (rice vermicelli)**
**1 ½ tablespoons neutral
 vegetable oil, divided**
1 medium onion, quartered and thinly sliced
3 cloves garlic, minced
3 cups bite-size broccoli florets
3 cups bite-size cauliflower florets
**2 cups fresh slender green beans,
 trimmed and cut in half**
**1 large red bell pepper, cut into
 narrow 2-inch strips**
1 to 2 fresh chilis, seeded and minced

Coconut-peanut sauce:
**½ cup natural peanut butter
 (smooth or chunky)**
¾ cup light coconut milk
Juice of 1 lime
2 tablespoons soy sauce or tamari
2 teaspoons grated fresh or bottled ginger
**½ teaspoon sriracha, or other
 hot sauce, to taste**
2 teaspoons agave nectar

Garnishes: (use any or all)
Chopped peanuts
Sliced scallions
Cilantro leaves

1   Cook the noodles according to package directions, then drain and cut into shorter lengths. Return the noodles to the pot and toss with about half of the oil, so that they don't stick to one another. Cover and set aside.

2   Heat the remaining oil in a soup pot. Add the onion and sauté over medium-low heat until translucent. Add the garlic and continue to sauté until both are golden.

3   Layer the broccoli, cauliflower, green beans, bell pepper, and chilis in the pot without stirring them in. Pour in a cup or so of water. Bring to a rapid simmer (you'll hear it rather than see it), then lower the heat. Cover and cook for 8 to 10 minutes, or until all the vegetables are tender-crisp.

4   Meanwhile, prepare the sauce. Combine the ingredients in a small mixing bowl and whisk together until completely blended. If the peanut butter is very dense, you might need to use a food processor or blender.

5   Add the sauce to the soup pot once the vegetables are tender-crisp to your liking. Stir everything together well. Bring to a gentle simmer and cook for 5 minutes longer, uncovered, or until the sauce has enveloped the vegetables.

6   To serve, place some of the noodles in the bottom of each bowl, and ladle some of the stew over them. Garnish with peanuts, scallions, and/or cilantro.

MIXED MUSHROOM & BOK CHOY SOUP

An aromatic broth with portobellos and crisp greens

This aromatic soup celebrates spring with lots of fresh bok choy, a favorite Asian green vegetable. This is an excellent way to whet the appetite for a vegetable stir-fry with rice or noodles.

1 recipe Dried Shiitake Mushroom Broth (page 14), with trimmed shiitake mushrooms

1 ½ cups cremini or white mushrooms, cleaned, stemmed, and sliced

2 fresh portobello mushrooms, about 4 inches in diameter, thinly sliced, then cut into bite-size pieces

¼ cup dry white wine, optional

5 to 6 stalks large bok choy or 2 to 3 baby bok choy, thinly sliced

3 to 4 scallions, white and green parts, sliced

2 to 3 tablespoons soy sauce or tamari, to taste

Freshly ground pepper to taste

1 Prepare the broth according to the recipe.

2 Once the broth is done, add the cremini and portobello mushrooms to it, then stir in the optional wine. Bring to a slow boil, then lower the heat. Simmer gently over low heat with the cover ajar for 10 minutes, or until the mushrooms are done but still pleasantly chewy.

3 Add the remaining ingredients and simmer for 5 to 8 minutes longer, or just until the bok choy is tender-crisp. Serve at once.

CHINESE CABBAGE & TOFU SOUP

An easy homemade version of the restaurant classic

4 to 6 servings

This light soup, served with Scallion Pancakes (page 17), is a perfect first course to serve before your favorite vegetable stir-fry.

1 tablespoon olive oil
1 large onion, quartered and thinly sliced
4 cups firmly packed, thinly
   sliced napa cabbage
1 cup thinly sliced small white
   or cremini mushrooms
15-ounce can baby corn, with liquid
Dried Shiitake Mushroom Broth (page 14)
   or a 32-ounce carton vegetable broth
2 tablespoons cooking sherry
   or white wine, optional
2 tablespoons soy sauce or
   tamari, or more, to taste
Freshly ground pepper to taste
1 cup snow peas, trimmed and halved
14-ounce tub firm tofu, cut into ½-inch dice

1   Heat the oil in a large soup pot. Add the onion and sauté over low heat until golden.

2   Add the remaining ingredients except the snow peas and tofu. Bring to a slow boil, then lower the heat. Simmer gently over low heat with the cover ajar for 10 minutes.

3   Remove from the heat. Stir in the snow peas and tofu and let the soup stand for 30 minutes, covered. Reheat and serve.

TOFU & SOBA NOODLE SOUP

Embellished with tender greens and shiitake mushrooms 6 servings

To enjoy this soup in the traditional way, slurp the noodles from the broth with chopsticks, then use an Asian soup spoon to scoop up what's left. This simple soup comes together in less than 30 minutes.

8-ounce package soba (buckwheat) noodles
32-ounce carton vegetable broth
8 to 10 large shiitake mushroom
   caps, stemmed and sliced
2 tablespoons soy sauce or tamari
1 tablespoon rice vinegar
2 teaspoons natural granulated sugar
2 to 3 teaspoons grated fresh or
   bottled ginger, to taste
3 scallions, thinly sliced
8 ounces soft or firm tofu
5 ounces baby spinach
1 cup chopped Asian greens (baby bok
   choy, tatsoi, or mizuna), optional
Freshly ground pepper to taste

1 Break the noodles in half and cook them in a large saucepan according to package directions until *al dente*, then drain. Rinse briefly with cool water.

2 Meanwhile, combine the broth, mushrooms, soy sauce, vinegar, sugar, and ginger in a soup pot. Bring to a slow boil, then lower the heat. Simmer gently over low heat with the cover ajar for 10 minutes.

3 Stir in the scallions, tofu, spinach, and optional greens. Cover and cook until the spinach is just wilted, about 2 minutes.

4 Stir in the noodles. Add about two cups of additional water, enough so that the broth isn't overly crowded. Season with pepper and additional soy sauce, if needed. Heat through and serve at once.

VIETNAMESE "BEEF" NOODLE SOUP

The classic *pho* made plant-based with seitan

This Asian soup is brimming with invigorating flavors and textures. I love it as a change of pace in the winter from thick soups and stews. It's still every bit as warming. Despite the length of the ingredient list, this is a quick soup—you'll be eating in about half an hour.

3- to 4-ounce bundle thin rice
    noodles or bean-thread noodles
1 tablespoon neutral vegetable oil
3 to 4 cloves garlic, minced
1 whole shallot or small onion, minced
6 cups water
2 vegetable bouillon cubes
2 tablespoons soy sauce or
    tamari, or more, to taste
2 teaspoons grated fresh or bottled
    ginger, or more, to taste
½ teaspoon five-spice powder, optional
2 cups water
6 to 8 ounces seitan or plant-based
    "beef," cut into thin strips
2 cups fresh mung bean sprouts
4 scallions, thinly sliced
¼ cup fresh cilantro leaves
2 teaspoons lime juice, or to taste
Freshly ground pepper to taste
Thinly sliced lime sections for garnish

1   Cook the noodles according to package directions until *al dente*, then drain and cut into shorter lengths suitable for soup. Set aside until needed.

2   Meanwhile, heat the oil in a soup pot. Add the garlic and shallot and sauté over medium-low heat until both are golden.

3   Add the water, bouillon cubes, soy sauce, ginger, optional five-spice powder, and water. Bring to a slow boil, then lower the heat. Simmer gently over low heat with the cover ajar for 10 minutes.

4   Add half of the bean sprouts, half of the scallions, and half of the cilantro. Season with lime juice and pepper. Taste to see if more soy sauce is needed. Simmer for 2 to 3 minutes longer, then remove from the heat.

5   Serve at once. Garnish the top of each serving with a thin wedge or two of lime along with the remaining bean sprouts, scallions, and cilantro.

SUMMER

When the appetite is dulled by summer's heat, nothing is more appealing than soups that make lavish use of garden vegetables, lush fruits, and fresh herbs. For the laziest and hottest days, you'll find soups that require no cooking at all and are best eaten chilled.

CREAM OF PEA & CUCUMBER SOUP

A cool green puree flavored with dill and lime   6 servings

This brightly colored soup makes a delightful introduction to a summer dinner, or it can be the centerpiece of a light meal, accompanied by salad-filled wraps. It needs little prep — everything just gets tossed into the blender.

2 long hothouse (English) or 3
   medium cucumbers (see Note)
16-ounce bag frozen green peas, thawed
13.5-ounce can light coconut milk
1 scallion, green parts only,
   coarsely chopped
¼ to ½ cup cilantro or parsley leaves
¼ cup chopped fresh dill (plus
   more, for garnish)
Juice of 1 lime, or more, to taste
1 teaspoon good quality curry powder
A few mint leaves, optional
Salt and freshly ground pepper to taste

1   See the Note below on whether to leave peels on the cucumbers. Either way, cut 1 ½ of the cucumbers into large chunks. Finely dice the remaining portion of cucumber to use for garnish, then set aside.

2   Place the cucumber chunks in a blender along with the peas, coconut milk, scallion, cilantro, dill, lime juice, curry powder, and optional mint. Process until smoothly blended.

3   Pour the soup into a serving container. Season with salt and pepper (this is a mild soup, so salt judiciously!). Taste to see if you'd like to add more lime juice.

4   Quarter lengthwise and thinly slice the reserved cucumber and stir it into the soup.

5   If time allows, refrigerate the soup for an hour or so to allow the flavors to meld. If the soup is too dense, stir in a little water, but let it stay fairly thick. Adjust the seasonings if need be.

6   Garnish each serving with a few peas, the reserved cucumber, and a sprig or two of dill.

NOTE   If using regular cucumbers, make sure they're unwaxed and organic. They should be crisp and flavorful, not watery and seedy. You can leave the peel on, but taste it first. If it's at all bitter, peel the cucumbers.

COOL AS A CUCUMBER SOUP

With lots of fresh herbs in a tangy, creamy base

4 to 6 servings

Here's an exceptionally easy no-cook soup. Inspired by the classic recipe for Middle Eastern cucumber soup, it's now possible to make vegan thanks to the much-improved generation of plant-based yogurts. My favorite is coconut yogurt, but use whatever kind you like best, as long as it's unsweetened.

2 large organic or hothouse cucumbers

12 ounces plain, unsweetened vegan yogurt

½ cup finely chopped mixed fresh herbs (try combining dill, parsley, and mint), or more, to taste

1 to 2 scallions, thinly sliced

1 ½ cups unsweetened plant-based milk, more or less, as needed

Juice of ½ lemon, or more to taste

½ teaspoon ground cumin, or more, to taste

Salt and freshly ground pepper to taste

1 Quarter the cucumbers lengthwise. If they contain watery seeds, cut most away and discard them. Either way, slice very thinly.

2 Transfer the sliced cucumbers to a serving container. Stir in the yogurt, herbs, scallions, and enough plant-based milk to give the soup a slightly thick consistency.

3 Season with lemon juice, cumin, salt, and pepper. Serve at once or refrigerate for an hour or two until chilled.

VARIATIONS For a heartier version of this soup, add a cup or so of cold, cooked barley or quinoa. And for a pleasantly peppery flavor, stir in a big handful or two of chopped watercress leaves (with some chopped stems).

COOL RATATOUILLE

The classic medley of eggplants, zucchini, and tomatoes   6 to 8 servings

This summery version of the classic stew makes use of summer's lush tomatoes and fresh herbs. Serve with slices of fresh whole-grain baguette or olive bread.

2 tablespoons extra-virgin olive oil

1 large red onion, chopped

3 to 4 cloves garlic, minced

1 cup water

2 medium eggplants (about 1 ½
   pounds total), peeled and diced

2 small zucchinis, sliced

4 cups diced ripe, juicy tomatoes

1 cup tomato sauce

¼ cup dry red wine, optional

1 to 2 teaspoons sweet or smoked paprika

¼ cup thinly sliced basil leaves,
   or more, to taste

¼ cup chopped fresh parsley

1 tablespoon fresh oregano
   leaves, or more, to taste

2 teaspoons fresh thyme
   leaves, or more, to taste

Salt and freshly ground pepper to taste

Vegan sour cream (homemade, page 7,
   or from an 8-ounce tub), optional

1   Heat the oil in a soup pot. Add the onion and sauté over medium-low heat until translucent. Add the garlic and continue to sauté until both are golden.

2   Add the water, eggplants, zucchinis, tomatoes, tomato sauce, optional wine, and paprika. Bring to a slow boil, then lower the heat. Simmer gently over low heat with the cover ajar until the vegetables are tender, but not overdone, about 25 minutes. Stir occasionally and make sure there is enough liquid to keep the vegetables moist. The consistency should be more like stew than soup.

3   Remove from the heat. Stir in the half of the basil and the remaining fresh herbs. Season with salt and pepper. Let the stew cool to room temperature.

4   To serve, garnish each serving with the remaining basil and, if desired, a dollop of sour cream.

LATE-SUMMER EGGPLANT STEW

With pasta, fresh and dried tomatoes, and olives

6 to 8 servings

Serve this Mediterranean-inspired stew with fresh corn on the cob and a simple green salad for a lovely summer dinner. For a larger meal, add a crusty bread and hummus.

2 tablespoons extra-virgin olive oil

1 medium onion, quartered and thinly sliced

2 to 3 cloves garlic, minced

3 cups water

2 medium eggplants (about 1 ½ pounds in all), cut into ½-inch dice

4 cups diced ripe tomatoes (try a mixture of red and yellow tomatoes)

½ cup finely chopped fresh parsley

1 tablespoon fresh oregano leaves, or 1 teaspoon dried

½ cup coarsely chopped cured black olives

½ cup oil-cured sun-dried tomatoes, sliced

Salt and freshly ground pepper to taste

1 cup uncooked small pasta, such as tiny shells or ditalini

8 to 12 fresh basil leaves, thinly sliced

1 Heat the oil in a soup pot. Add the onion and sauté over medium-low heat until translucent. Add the garlic and continue to sauté until both are golden.

2 Add the water and eggplant. Bring to a slow boil, then lower the heat. Simmer gently over low heat with the cover ajar until the eggplant is just tender, about 15 minutes.

3 Stir the tomatoes into the soup pot, followed by half of the parsley and the oregano. Return to a gentle simmer, then cook for 8 to 10 minutes longer, or until the eggplant is completely tender.

4 Stir in the olives and dried tomatoes. Season with salt and pepper. Remove from the heat and let stand, covered.

5 Cook the pasta in a separate saucepan until *al dente*, then drain.

6 Stir the cooked pasta into the soup and adjust the consistency with more water, if need be. The consistency should be more like a stew than soup.

7 Serve hot, warm, or even at room temperature. Garnish each serving with a sprinkling of the remaining parsley, and the basil.

GARDEN GREENS SOUP

Leafy vegetables and herbs with a sprinkling of couscous

A soup that looks and tastes garden-fresh, this is a good one to serve on cooler summer evenings

⅓ cup couscous, preferably whole grain

1 ½ tablespoons olive oil

2 medium onions, quartered
   and thinly sliced

2 to 3 cloves garlic, minced

32-ounce container vegetable
   broth or 4 cups water with 2
   vegetable bouillon cubes

½ small head napa or savoy
   cabbage, thinly shredded

5 ounces baby spinach (or any
   other spinach variety, stemmed,
   chopped and well rinsed)

2 cups shredded lettuce, any variety

2 medium tomatoes, finely diced

¼ cup chopped fresh parsley

2 to 3 tablespoons minced fresh dill

3 scallions, thinly sliced

1 teaspoon good quality curry powder

Juice of ½ lemon

Salt and freshly ground pepper to taste

1 Place the couscous in a heatproof container and cover with ⅔ cup boiling water. Cover and let stand until needed.

2 Heat the oil in a soup pot. Add the onions and sauté over medium-low heat until translucent. Add the garlic and continue to sauté until both are golden.

3 Add the remaining ingredients except the salt and pepper. Bring to a slow boil, then lower the heat. Simmer gently over low heat with the cover ajar for 8 to 10 minutes, or until the vegetables are just tender.

4 Remove from the heat and stir in the cooked couscous. Adjust the consistency with about 2 cups water, more or less as needed, to give the soup a dense but not overly crowded consistency.

5 Season with salt and pepper. Serve at once or allow the soup to cool until warm or room temperature before serving.

TANGY COLD POTATO SPINACH SOUP

A compatible pair of vegetables in a cool, creamy base   6 to 8 servings

Here's a cold soup that's substantial, as well as refreshing. Serve with fresh flatbread and tabbouleh salad for a tasty summer meal.

5 to 6 medium potatoes, peeled and diced

32-ounce carton vegetable broth or 4 cups
    water with 2 vegetable bouillon cubes

5 ounces baby spinach

1 ½ cups unsweetened plant-based
    milk, or more, as needed

¼ cup chopped fresh parsley

2 to 3 scallions, white and
    green parts, sliced

2 tablespoons minced fresh
    dill, or more, to taste

Juice of ½ to 1 lemon, to taste

Vegan Sour Cream (page 7), or an
    8-ounce tub vegan sour cream

Salt and freshly ground pepper to taste

1 Combine the potatoes with the broth in a large soup pot. Bring to a simmer, then lower the heat. Simmer gently over low heat with the cover ajar until the potatoes are tender, about 15 minutes. Remove from the heat.

2 With a slotted spoon, transfer a heaping cup of the potato dice to a shallow bowl or plate, mash well, and stir back into the soup. Stir in the spinach and cook for a minute or two longer, until just wilted. Remove from the heat.

3 Stir the remaining ingredients, except for the sour cream, salt, and pepper, into the soup pot.

4 Allow the soup to cool to room temperature, then stir in the sour cream. Season with salt and pepper. Cover and refrigerate for a few hours or overnight to chill thoroughly before serving.

COLD CREAMY LEEK & POTATO SOUP

A luscious, plant-based take on a classic

Delicious served chilled in the summer, this leek and potato soup is inspired by the classic vichyssoise. Vegan sour cream or yogurt provide the creamy base. Make sure to rinse the leeks carefully to get all the grit from between the layers!

2 tablespoons olive oil

2 medium onions, chopped

2 to 3 cloves garlic, minced

4 large or 6 medium potatoes (any variety), peeled and diced

2 teaspoons salt-free seasoning (see page 8 for brands)

2 large or 3 medium leeks, white and palest green parts only, cut in half lengthwise, then into half-rings crosswise, and rinsed very well

1 medium red bell pepper, finely diced

3 to 4 ounces baby arugula

1 ½ cups unsweetened plant-based milk, or as needed

Vegan Sour Cream (page 7), 8-ounce tub vegan sour cream, or 8 ounces plain vegan yogurt, divided

¼ cup minced fresh dill, plus more for garnish

Salt and freshly ground pepper to taste

1   Heat the oil in a soup pot. Add the onion and sauté over medium-low heat until translucent. Add the garlic and continue to sauté until both are golden.

2   Add the potatoes, seasoning, and enough water to cover all but about ½ inch of the vegetables. Bring to a slow boil, then lower the heat. Simmer gently over low heat with the cover ajar until the potatoes are tender, about 20 minutes. Remove from the heat and let cool to room temperature.

3   Place the leeks in a skillet with about ½ inch of water. Cover and sweat over medium heat for 5 minutes, stirring occasionally. Add the bell pepper and continue to sweat until both vegetables are just tender. Add the arugula and cover. Cook just until wilted down, about 1 to 2 minutes. Remove from the heat.

4   Transfer the potato-onion mixture to a food processor or blender. Add the plant-based milk and puree until smooth. Return to the soup pot, then stir in half of the sour cream. Or, skip the food processor and insert an immersion blender into the pot and blend the soup until pureed to your liking.

5   Stir the leek mixture into the soup pot. Adjust the consistency with more plant-based milk, if needed, to give the soup a medium-thick consistency.

6   Stir in the dill and season with salt and pepper. Let the soup cool to room temperature, then cover and chill completely for a few hours or overnight before serving. Top each serving with more sour cream and dill.

CREAM OF LETTUCE SOUP

With a variety of fresh summer herbs

Have you ever bought a head (or two) of lettuce, only to discover that there's already some in the fridge? Or, is your own garden or farm share yielding more than you know what to do with? This recipe turns this dilemma into an opportunity to enjoy a simple, garden-fresh soup.

1 ½ tablespoons olive oil

2 medium onions, chopped

3 to 4 cloves garlic, minced

32-ounce container vegetable broth
   or 4 cups water with 2
   vegetable bouillon cubes

10 cups coarsely chopped lettuce,
   any variety or combination

½ cup minced fresh herbs (choose from a
   mixture of chives, dill, oregano, basil,
   and parsley), plus more for garnish

12.3-ounce package firm silken
   tofu, or a 15-ounce can cannellini
   beans, drained and rinsed

1 cup unsweetened plant-based
   milk, or more, as needed

Juice of ½ lemon, or more, to taste

Salt and freshly ground pepper to taste

Vegan sour cream (homemade, page 7,
   or from an 8-ounce tub), optional

1 Heat the oil in a soup pot. Add the onions and sauté over medium-low heat until golden. Add the the garlic and continue to sauté until the onions are lightly browned.

2 Add the broth and 8 cups of the lettuce, reserving the rest. Bring to a slow boil, then lower the heat. Simmer gently over low heat with the cover ajar for 10 minutes. Stir in the herbs and remove from the heat.

3 With a slotted spoon, transfer the solid ingredients to a food processor or blender, along with the tofu, and puree (in batches if necessary), until smooth. Return to the soup pot. Or, skip the food processor and insert an immersion blender into the pot and blend the soup until pureed to your liking.

4 Stir in enough plant-based milk to give the soup a slightly thick consistency. Season with lemon juice, salt, and pepper. This mild soup needs good amount of each to heighten the flavor.

5 Cut the reserved lettuce into thin shreds and stir into the pot.

6 Allow the soup to cool to room temperature, then chill in the refrigerator for at least an hour before serving.

7 Top each serving with extra fresh herbs, plus a dollop of sour cream, if desired.

COOL ZUCCHINI CARROT SOUP

In a white bean and silken tofu base   6 servings

This refreshing cold soup is a good choice for a
summer company meal. A colorful pasta salad
and grilled vegetables complete a festive warm
weather meal.

1 tablespoon olive oil
1 medium onion, quartered and thinly sliced
2 medium carrots, peeled and grated
    (or 1 cup pre-grated carrots)
2 medium zucchinis, grated or spiralized
    (cut spirals into shorter pieces)
12.3-ounce package firm silken tofu
15-ounce can Great Northern or
    cannellini beans, drained and rinsed
¼ cup chopped fresh parsley
3 to 4 cups unsweetened plant-
    based milk, or as needed
2 teaspoons good-quality curry powder
2 tablespoons minced fresh dill
Juice of ½ to 1 lemon, to taste
Salt and freshly ground pepper to taste

1   Heat the oil in a medium skillet. Add the onion
and sauté over medium-low heat until golden.

2   Add the carrots and just enough water to keep
the bottom of the skillet moist. Cover and cook over
medium heat for 3 minutes. Add the zucchini and
continue to cook, covered, until the carrot and zucchini are tender but not overdone, about 3 minutes
longer. Uncover and set aside until needed.

3   Combine the tofu, half of the beans, the parsley,
and 1 cup of the plant-based milk in a food processor or blender. Process until smoothly pureed.

4   Transfer the puree to a serving container. Stir
in the carrot and zucchini mixture, the remaining
beans, and enough additional plant-based milk to
give the soup a flowing, medium-thick consistency.
Stir in the curry and dill, then season with lemon
juice, salt, and pepper.

5   Let the soup to stand for an hour or so to allow
the flavors to meld. Serve just warm or at room
temperature. Or, refrigerate until chilled, and serve
cold.

COLD TOMATO MANGO COCONUT SOUP

Summer vegetables and a lush fruit in a coconut broth   6 servings

---

Think of this no-cook soup as a Thai-flavored gazpacho. It's best made with ripe, flavorful summer tomatoes. Serve with a cold noodle dish for a quick warm-weather meal.

**4 medium ripe tomatoes,
    finely diced (see Note)**
1 ripe mango, finely diced (any variety)
**½ medium cucumber, peeled,
    seeded, and finely diced**
½ medium red bell pepper, finely diced
2 scallions, thinly sliced
¼ cup chopped cilantro, or more, to taste
**1 small fresh hot chili pepper,
    seeded and minced, optional**
Two 13.5-ounce cans light coconut milk
1 teaspoon good quality curry powder
½ cup jarred Thai peanut satay sauce
2 to 3 tablespoons lime juice, to taste
Salt and freshly ground pepper to taste

1 Combine all ingredients in a serving container and stir together. Cover and refrigerate for an hour or two, until chilled.

2 Taste and adjust the seasonings before serving.

NOTE When cutting up the tomatoes, feel free to discard some of the seedy parts.

COLD ZUCCHINI CORN SOUP

A refreshing summer chowder

Zucchini and corn are an appealing pairing in a fresh summer chowder. Serve with croutons or crisp tortilla strips to add a pleasant crunch.

1 tablespoon olive oil
1 medium onion, chopped
2 cloves garlic, minced
3 medium zucchini, cut into ½-inch dice
4 cups lightly cooked fresh corn kernels
   (from 4 to 5 good-sized ears)
4 cups water
1 vegetable bouillon cube
¼ cup chopped fresh parsley
1 teaspoon ground cumin
1 ½ cups unsweetened plant-based
   milk, or more, as needed
2 tablespoons lemon juice, or more, to taste
Salt and freshly ground pepper to taste

Garnishes (use any or all)
Garlic Croutons or Crispy
   Tortilla Strips (page 25)
Thinly sliced fresh basil leaves, as desired
Vegan sour cream (homemade, page 7,
   or from an 8-ounce tub)

1   Heat the oil in a soup pot. Add the onion and sauté over medium-low heat until translucent. Add the garlic and continue to sauté until both are golden.

2   Set aside half of the zucchini dice and half of the corn kernels. Add the remainder to the soup pot followed by the water, bouillon cube, parsley, and cumin. Bring to a slow boil, then lower the heat. Simmer gently over low heat with the cover ajar until the zucchini is just tender, about 8 minutes.

3   With a slotted spoon, transfer the solid ingredients to a food processor or blender with a little of the cooking liquid and puree until smooth. Return to the soup pot. Or skip the food processor and insert an immersion blender into the pot and blend the soup. Leave a little texture, if you'd like.

4   Place the reserved zucchini and corn in a medium skillet with a little water. Cover and steam until both are just tender. Stir into the pureed soup.

5   Add enough plant-based milk to give the soup a medium-thick consistency. Stir in lemon juice, salt, and pepper. Allow to cool to room temperature, then chill in the refrigerator for a few hours.

6   Serve cold with the garnishes of your choice.

CREAM OF CORN & WATERCRESS SOUP

With a sprinkling of fresh oregano

The peppery flavor of watercress provides a delightful contrast to the sweetness of summer corn in a simple soup. Try using Butter and Sugar corn (with yellow and white kernels) for a nice touch.

6 medium ears fresh sweet corn

2 tablespoons olive oil

2 large onions, chopped

2 cloves garlic, minced

2 medium potatoes, peeled and diced

**2 cups watercress, mostly leaves,
   some chopped stems**

**2 cups unsweetened plant-
   based milk, or as needed**

Salt and freshly ground pepper

**1 tablespoon fresh oregano
   leaves, or more, to taste**

1 Cook the corn in plenty of rapidly simmering water until the kernels are just tender, then remove the corn with tongs and reserve the cooking water. When the corn is cool enough to handle, scrape the kernels off the cobs with a sharp knife. Set the kernels aside.

2 Heat the oil in a soup pot. Add the onions and sauté over medium-low heat until translucent. Add the garlic and continue to sauté until both are golden.

3 Add the potatoes and 4 cups of the cooking liquid from the corn. Bring to a slow boil, then lower the heat. Simmer gently over low heat with the cover ajar for 10 minutes. Add half of the watercress. Simmer until the potatoes are tender, about 10 minutes longer, then remove from the heat.

4 Set aside a cup of the corn kernels and puree the remainder in a food processor or blender until fairly smooth. Transfer the puree to a bowl.

5 Transfer the solid ingredients from the soup to a food processor or blender and puree until smooth. Return the puree to the soup pot, along with the corn puree, the reserved corn kernels, and the reserved watercress.

6 Return to low heat and stir in enough plant-based milk to give the soup a slightly thick consistency. Season with salt and pepperr.

7 Let the soup cool to room temperature, then refrigerate until chilled. Top each serving with a sprinkling of oregano.

TORTILLA SOUP WITH SUMMER SQUASH

A hot soup for cool summer nights

6 servings

There are many variations this classic South-western soup (not all of which are vegan). One constant is the addition of corn tortillas, cut into strips and cooked on the stovetop or baked until crisp. This plant-rich version can be enjoyed any time of year, though it's especially welcome in late summer, when squashes and fresh corn are abundant.

1 tablespoon olive oil

1 large onion, chopped

2 to 3 cloves garlic, minced

5 cups water

1 medium bell pepper, any color, diced

2 medium zucchini or yellow
    squash, or 1 of each, diced

14.5-ounce can fire roasted diced tomatoes

15-ounce can tomato sauce

2 cups fresh corn kernels, from 2 to 3 ears

1 or 2 fresh jalapeños, seeded and
    finely chopped (see Variation)

2 teaspoons ground cumin

2 teaspoons all-purpose seasoning blend

Salt and freshly ground pepper to taste

Garnish

6 regular-size corn tortillas or
    12 mini corn tortillas

¼ to ½ cup fresh cilantro leaves

1 medium avocado, peeled and sliced

1   Heat the oil in a soup pot. Add the onion and sauté over medium-low heat until translucent. Add the garlic and continue to sauté until both are golden.

2   Add the water along with the remaining ingredients except the salt and pepper. Bring to a slow boil, then lower the heat. Simmer gently over low heat with the cover ajar for 10 minutes.

3   Adjust the consistency with a little more water if the soup is crowded. Season with salt and pepper.

4   While the soup cooks, cut the tortillas into strips about ¼ inch wide by 2 inches long. Heat a large skillet (spray with a little cooking oil spray or coat with a little olive oil) and add the tortilla strips. Toast in the skillet over medium-high heat, stirring frequently, until dry and crisp, then remove to a plate to cool.

5   Garnish each serving with some of the tortilla strips, cilantro, and a few slices of avocado.

VARIATIONS

To make this soup a main dish, add about 3 cups of cooked or canned (drained and rinsed) pinto or black beans in step 3.

For a milder soup, use 1 or 2 fresh poblano peppers, seeded and finely chopped.

CORN PUREE WITH SAUTÉED PEPPERS

With plenty of onion and garlic

An appetizing soup designed to impress summer guests—or your own family!

6 large ears fresh sweet corn

3 tablespoons extra-virgin olive oil, divided

2 large onions, chopped

4 cloves garlic, minced

Pinch of cayenne pepper or dried
   hot red pepper flakes

1 to 1 ½ cups unsweetened plant-
   based milk, or more, as needed

2 tablespoons lemon or lime juice

Salt and freshly ground pepper to taste

1 each red, orange, and green bell
   peppers, cut into short narrow strips

Sliced fresh basil leaves, chopped
   fresh parsley, or fresh oregano
   leaves for garnish, as desired

1 Cook the corn in plenty of rapidly simmering water until the kernels are just tender. Remove the corn with tongs and reserve the cooking water. When the corn is cool enough to handle, scrape the kernels off the cobs with a sharp knife. Set aside 1 cup of the corn kernels.

2 Heat half of the oil in a soup pot. Add the onion and sauté over medium-low heat until translucent. Add the garlic and continue to sauté until both are golden.

3 Transfer the onions and garlic to a food processor and process with the corn kernels (except for the reserved cup), in batches if necessary, until smoothly pureed. Transfer back to the soup pot.

4 Stir in 4 cups of the cooking water from the corn. Bring to a slow boil, then lower the heat. Add the cayenne pepper and enough plant-based milk to give the soup a slightly thick consistency.

5 Simmer gently over low heat with the cover ajar for 10 minutes. Stir in the lemon juice and season with salt and pepper. Allow the soup to stand off the heat, uncovered, for about an hour.

6 Heat the remaining oil in a large skillet or stir-fry pan. Add the bell peppers and sauté over medium heat until they're touched with golden-brown here and there. Transfer to a plate to allow them to cool.

7 Serve the soup warm or at room temperature. Garnish each serving with some bell pepper and fresh herb of your choice.

FRESH TOMATO SOUP WITH CORN SAUCE

A midsummer night's feast

6 servings

This cold soup is as appealing to look at as it is to eat. Use lush, ripe (or even overripe) tomatoes for best results. Serve with fresh bread and follow with a grain-based salad (quinoa tabbouli, for example) for a light summer meal.

2 tablespoons extra-virgin olive oil

2 large onions, chopped

2 cloves garlic, minced

2 large celery stalks, peeled and diced

2 cups water

2 pounds ripe tomatoes, coarsely chopped

2 tablespoons chopped fresh dill

1 teaspoon salt-free seasoning
  (see page 8 for brands)

4 ears fresh corn

½ cup unsweetened plant-based milk

1 ½ to 2 cups tomato juice, preferably
  low-sodium, or as needed

1 tablespoon lemon juice, or more, to taste

Salt and freshly ground pepper to taste

Fresh herb or herbs (parsley, cilantro, dill,
  oregano, or a combination) for garnish

1 Heat the oil in a soup pot. Add the onions, garlic, and celery and sauté over medium-low heat until all are golden.

2 Add the water and tomatoes. Bring to a slow boil, then lower the heat. Simmer gently over low heat with the cover ajar for 10 minutes.

3 Add the dill and salt-free seasoning, and simmer for 5 minutes longer. Remove from the heat and allow to cool to room temperature, uncovered.

4 Meanwhile, cook the corn until just tender, then drain and allow it to cool. When cool enough to handle, scrape the kernels off the cobs with a sharp knife. Combine the corn kernels with the plant-based milk in a food processor or blender and process until smoothly pureed. Transfer to a covered container and refrigerate until needed.

5 Once the tomato mixture has cooled, puree it in batches in a food processor or blender until smoothly pureed, then return to the soup pot. Or skip the food processor and insert an immersion blender into the pot and blend the soup until pureed to your liking.

6 Add enough tomato juice to give the soup a slightly thick consistency. Stir in the lemon juice and season with salt and pepper. Refrigerate until chilled.

7 To serve, fill each bowl about ¾ full with the tomato soup. Place a ladleful of the sweet corn sauce in the center of each bowl, and garnish each serving with a sprinkling of fresh herbs.

QUICK COOL PINTO BEAN PUREE

With tomatoes, peppers, and olives   6 servings

With the help of a food processor, this tasty, no-cook soup is ready to eat in minutes. Serve with stone-ground tortilla chips or warmed flour tortillas.

3 to 3 ½ cups cooked or two 15-ounce
   cans pinto beans, drained and rinsed
14.5-ounce can fire roasted diced tomatoes
2 scallions, coarsely chopped,
   plus extra for garnish
¼ cup fresh cilantro leaves
Juice of 1 lime
1 teaspoon chili powder
1 teaspoon ground cumin
1 medium green bell pepper,
   cut into large chunks
4 ripe plum tomatoes, cut into large chunks
½ cup pitted black olives
¼ cup seeded and chopped mild green chilis
   (like poblano or Anaheim), optional
1 ½ cups water, more or less, as needed
Peeled and diced avocado for garnish
Vegan Sour Cream (page 7, or
   from an 8-ounce tub) for
   garnish as desired, optional

1   Combine the beans, canned tomatoes, scallions, and cilantro in a food processor and process until pureed, leaving just a bit of texture. Transfer to a large serving container and stir in the lime juice, chili powder, and cumin.

2   Place the bell pepper and fresh tomatoes in the food processor and pulse on and off 2 or 3 times.

3   Add the olives and pulse on and off quickly, 2 or 3 times more, or until the vegetables are coarsley chopped. Take care not to over-process. Stir into the bean puree, then add the chilis, if desired.

4   Stir in enough water to give the soup a medium-thick consistency. Serve at once or cover and refrigerate until needed.

5   Garnish each serving with diced avocado, additional scallions (thinly sliced), and optional sour cream.

CREAMY AVOCADO SOUP

With red bell pepper and fresh herbs

4 to 6 servings

This quick, easy no-cook soup is perfectly refreshing on a hot summer day. It's best eaten the same day as it's made, since avocado discolors and doesn't keep well. Serve as first course for Southwestern specialties like vegan burritos, enchiladas, or tacos.

2 large ripe avocados, pitted and peeled
Juice of ½ lemon, or more, to taste
Vegan Sour Cream (page 7), or an
    8-ounce tub vegan sour cream
2 cups unsweetened plant-based milk,
    more or less as needed
1 teaspoon ground cumin
½ teaspoon good-quality curry powder
Salt and freshly ground pepper to taste

Garnish
1 medium red bell pepper, finely diced
1 to 2 fresh hot or mild green chilis,
    seeded and finelychopped
2 scallions, green parts only, thinly sliced
¼ cup chopped fresh cilantro or parsley

1 Dice enough avocado to make 1 cup, then mash the remainder well. Combine the diced and mashed avocados in a serving container and mix immediately with the lemon juice.

2 Stir in the sour cream, then enough plant-based milk to give the soup a slightly thick consistency.

3 Stir in the cumin and curry powder, then season with salt and pepper. Cover and refrigerate for 1 to 2 hours, or until chilled.

4 Combine the garnish ingredients in a small bowl and stir together. After ladling the soup into bowls, distribute the garnish among them.

CLASSIC GAZPACHO

The garden-fresh no-cook classic

A collection of vegan soups wouldn't be complete without this Spanish classic. It's especially delicious topped with Garlic Croutons (page 25).

Soup base
2 cups coarsely chopped ripe tomatoes
⅔ large cucumber, peeled and
   cut into chunks
⅔ large green or red bell pepper,
   cut into chunks
2 scallions, green parts only,
   cut into several pieces
Handful of parsley or cilantro sprigs

To finish the soup
3 cups tomato juice, preferably low-
   sodium or salt-free, or as needed
⅓ large cucumber, peeled and finely diced
⅓ large green or red bell pepper, finely diced
2 ripe tomatoes, finely diced
1 large carrot, peeled and finely diced
Juice of ½ to 1 lemon, to taste
2 teaspoons chili powder, or to taste
Dried hot red pepper flakes or other
   hot seasoning to taste, optional
Salt and freshly ground pepper to taste

1   Combine all the ingredients for the base in a food processor or blender and puree until fairly smooth.

2   Transfer the puree to a serving container. Stir in enough tomato juice to give the soup a slightly thick consistency.

3   Stir in the remaining ingredients. Cover and refrigerate for at least an hour before serving.

TOMATO & WATERMELON GAZPACHO

A fruity twist on traditional gazpacho   6 servings

Adding summer fruit to classic gazpacho works surprisingly well. The sweet and piquant flavors of watermelon and tomatoes play off of one another in this palate-pleasing summer soup.

Soup base
2 cups coarsely chopped ripe tomatoes
2 heaping cups coarsely chopped
  seedless watermelon
½ medium red bell pepper
⅔ large cucumber, peeled
  and cut into chunks
2 scallions, green parts only,
  cut into several pieces

To finish the soup
1 cup diced ripe tomatoes or halved
  cherry or grape tomatoes
2 cups finely diced seedless watermelon
½ medium red bell pepper, finely diced
⅓ large cucumber, peeled and finely diced
Juice of ½ to 1 lemon or lime, to taste
Pinch of salt
Freshly ground pepper to taste
Sliced fresh basil or small basil
  leaves for garnish

1 Combine the base ingredients in a food processor or blender. Puree until fairly smooth, leaving some texture.

2 Transfer the puree to a serving container. Add the remaining ingredients (except basil) and stir together.

3 Cover and refrigerate for at least an hour before serving to chill and allow the flavors to blend.

4 Garnish each serving with basil.

VARIATION Add a pitted and diced ripe peach or nectarine (or two) to the gazpacho.

ZESTY GREEN GAZPACHO

Summary vegetables enlivened with Southwestern flavors

This tomatillo-flavored gazpacho can be eaten as soon as it's made, but it benefits from an hour or so of chilling time to allow the lively flavors to mingle. It's a fantastic first course for a Mexican or Southwestern-style meal.

2 large cucumbers, peeled, quartered
   lengthwise, and seeded
½ yellow or orange bell pepper
½ medium head tender lettuce,
   coarsely chopped
2 scallions, coarsely chopped
⅓ cup fresh cilantro leaves
1 cup hulled and coarsely chopped fresh
   tomatillos (or ¾ cup jarred salsa verde)
1 mild or hot fresh green chili,
   seeded and minced
Juice of 1 lime
1 teaspoon ground cumin
Salt and freshly ground pepper to taste

Garnish
½ yellow or orange pepper, finely diced
1 medium avocado, peeled and finely diced
1 medium mango, pitted and finely
   diced, or 2 peaches or nectarines,
   pitted and finely diced
Fresh basil leaves, whole or sliced

1   Combine all the ingredients, except the garnishes, in a blender or food processor. Process until pureed, leaving a little texture. Transfer to a large serving container.

2   Cover and refrigerate for an hour or more, until chilled.

3   Combine the garnish ingredients in a small bowl and stir together. Top each serving of soup with some of the garnish mixture.

CORN & YELLOW TOMATO GAZPACHO

A midsummer bowl of sunshine

Two midsummer vegetables at the peak of their flavor join forces in a refreshing cold soup. Though this is an impressive first course for company, you need not wait until you have guests to make it, especially if you have a surplus of yellow tomatoes.

1 tablespoon olive oil
1 large or 2 medium onions, chopped
2 to 3 cloves garlic, finely chopped
4 cups fresh corn kernels, 1 cup reserved
2 pints yellow cherry tomatoes,
   1 cup reserved
Juice of 1 lemon, or to taste
Salt and freshly ground pepper to taste

Garnish
Reserved corn kernels (lightly steamed)
Reserved yellow cherry tomatoes, sliced
½ cup red cherry or grape tomatoes, sliced
½ cup finely diced cucumber
Basil, cilantro, or oregano leaves
1 jalapeño pepper, seeded and
   thinly sliced, optional

1 Heat the oil in a wide skillet or stir-fry pan. Add the onions and sauté over medium-low heat until translucent. Add the garlic and continue to sauté until both are golden brown.

2 Add 3 cups of the corn kernels to the skillet, along with about ¼ cup water. Cover and cook until the corn is tender-crisp, about 3 minutes.

3 Transfer the onion and corn mixture to a food processor or blender, along with the yellow tomatoes (make sure to reserve 1 cup of them). Add about 1 cup water and blend until smooth.

4 Transfer the corn puree to a serving container. Stir in the lemon juice and season with salt and pepper.

5 Cover and refrigerate the puree for an hour or two until chilled. It may thicken a bit; add a little more water, as needed, for a medium-thick consistency.

6 Just before serving, combine the reserved corn kernels, yellow tomatoes, red tomatoes, cucumber, and fresh herbs in a small bowl. Add the jalapeño if using and toss together.

7 Top each bowlful with some of the garnish.

SPICED SUMMER FRUIT SOUP

Berries, stone fruits, and grapes in a wine-scented base

6 or more servings

This, and the following berry soup, are the only fruit soups in this chapter that need a bit of cooking. The wine and spices give it a wonderfully complex flavor.

1 cup fresh blueberries
1 cup hulled and chopped strawberries
3 sweet red plums or pluots, diced
4 medium ripe peaches, diced
1 cup seedless red or green grapes
Juice of ½ lemon
4 cups apple or white grape juice
Cinnamon stick
5 whole cloves
⅓ cup semisweet red wine
2 to 3 tablespoons natural granulated
   sugar, maple syrup, or agave, to taste
Mint leaves for garnish

1 Combine all the ingredients in a soup pot. Bring to a slow boil, then lower the heat. Simmer gently over low heat with the cover ajar for 20 minutes, or until the fruit is tender.

2 Allow the soup to cool, then refrigerate for several hours or overnight until chilled. If too crowded, adjust the consistency with more apple juice.

3 Remove the cinnamon stick and cloves before serving. Garnish each serving with a few mint leaves.

CHILLED BERRY SOUP

A medley of blueberries, strawberries, and raspberries

6 servings

Late-season strawberries and midsummer berries converge in a sweetly spiced broth.

1 pint blueberries
1 pint strawberries, hulled
   and coarsely chopped
1 cup raspberries
2 medium peaches or nectarines, chopped
4 cups bottled organic strawberry
   or raspberry juice
¼ cup dry red or white wine, optional
Juice of ½ lemon
1 teaspoon ground cinnamon
½ teaspoon ground allspice
¼ teaspoon ground nutmeg
Natural granulated sugar, maple
   syrup, or agave to taste, if needed
Sliced strawberries for garnish
Mint leaves for garnish

1 Combine all the ingredients except the last two in a soup pot. Bring to a slow boil, then lower the heat. Simmer gently over low heat with the cover ajar for 10 to 15 minutes, or until the fruit is tender. Remove from the heat.

2 Taste the soup, and if you'd like it sweeter, add a sweetener of your choice. Depending on the sweetness of the fruit and the fruit juice, you may not need to added sweetener at all, or very little.

3 Allow the soup to cool to room temperature, then refrigerate for several hours or overnight until chilled. Garnish each serving with a few strawberry slices and mint leaves.

STRAWBERRY COLADA SOUP

A celebration of strawberries in creamy coconut milk

This super-quick no-cook soup is luscious enough to serve for dessert.

**1 ½ cups bottled organic strawberry
  or raspberry juice**
13.5-ounce can light coconut milk
**1 quart ripe, sweet organic strawberries,
  washed, hulls trimmed away, and cut
  into approximately ½-inch chunks**
**1 to 2 tablespoons agave or
  maple syrup, to taste**
¼ teaspoon ground cinnamon
Fresh mint leaves for garnish, optional

1 Combine the strawberry juice and coconut milk in a serving container and whisk together.

2 Crush a scant cup of the strawberries, then stir into the strawberry juice and coconut milk mixture, followed by the cut strawberries.

3 Sweeten as desired, then whisk in the cinnamon. Refrigerate for an hour or so before serving. If desired, garnish each serving with a few mint leaves.

CHILLED CANTALOUPE SOUP

Enhanced with mango and lime juice 6 servings

It takes minutes to make this sweet soup. Try serving it after a spicy meal —it's a wonderful palate cooler.

8 heaping cups lush, ripe cantaloupe,
    cut into 2-inch chunks
1 ½ cups bottled mango nectar
    or orange-mango juice
1 to 2 tablespoons lime juice
2 to 3 tablespoons agave or
    maple syrup, to taste
Pinch of cinnamon
Pinch of nutmeg
1 cup berries, any variety, for garnish
Mint leaves for garnish, optional

1 Set aside about 2 cups of the cantaloupe chunks and place the rest in a blender. Process until smoothly pureed, then add the juices, agave, and spices. Process again until thoroughly blended, then transfer to a serving container.

2 Cut the reserved melon chunks into ½-inch dice and stir them into the soup. Cover and chill for an hour or so before serving. Garnish each serving with some berries and a few mint leaves, if desired.

MINTED PEACH SOUP

Creamy and juicy, with a hint of ginger

For this fruit soup, don't settle for less than luscious, tree-ripened peaches. Avoid peaches that are purchased rock-hard, only to ripen to flavorless mush after several days of waiting.

2 ½ pounds ripe, juicy peaches, pitted
2 cups bottled peach, pear, or mango nectar
½ cup unsweetened plant-based milk
½ cup vanilla plant-based creamer
1 teaspoon vanilla extract
½ to 1 teaspoon grated fresh or
    bottled ginger, to taste
Pinch of nutmeg
2 tablespoons crushed fresh mint
    leaves or 1 mint tea bag
1 to 2 tablespoons agave or
    maple syrup, to taste
Fresh mint leaves for garnish, optional

1 Dice about 2 cups of the peaches and set aside. Place the rest in a food processor or blender with the juice. Process until smoothly pureed, then transfer to a serving container.

2 Stir in the plant-based milk, creamer, vanilla extract, and spices.

3 In a heatproof cup, steep the fresh mint leaves or mint tea in about ½ cup boiling water for 10 to 15 minutes. Strain, then stir into the serving container.

4 Stir in the reserved peaches and add agave to taste. Refrigerate for an hour or two to allow the flavors to blend.

5 Just before serving, adjust the consistency with more fruit nectar if too dense. Garnish each bowlful with a few fresh mint leaves, if desired.

MELON MEDLEY SOUP

A trio of melons in a classic vanilla and orange base

A perfect dessert soup to make in July and August, when melons are at their sweetest. This makes a refreshing finish to a meal of grilled vegetables and plant proteins.

**3 cups seedless watermelon,
  cut into ½-inch dice**
**3 cups honeydew melon, cut
  into ½-inch dice**
1 medium cantaloupe, cut into large chunks
1 pint vanilla vegan ice cream
2 cups orange juice, preferably fresh
Blueberries for garnish
Mint leaves for garnish

1 Combine the watermelon and honeydew in a bowl. Place the cantaloupe chunks in a separate bowl. Cover both bowls and chill for an hour or more.

2 Just before serving, combine the cantaloupe, ice cream, and orange juice in a food processor or blender, and process, in batches if need be, until smoothly pureed.

3 To serve, divide among 6 bowls. Place about 1 cup of the watermelon and honeydew mixture in each. Scatter some blueberries over the top of each bowlful and garnish with several mint leaves.

VANILLA FRUIT CUP SOUP

A colorful fruit salad transformed into a dessert soup

6 servings

Requiring no cooking or blending, this soup takes full advantage of lush midsummer fruits.

2 cups berries, as desired
(blueberries, raspberries,
blackberries, or a combination)
½ medium cantaloupe, cut into ½-inch dice
2 cups seedless watermelon,
cut into ½-inch dice
1 ½ cups green seedless grapes,
whole if small or halved if large
2 peaches or nectarines, pitted
and cut into ½-inch dice
2 cups vanilla vegan yogurt
1 teaspoon vanilla extract
1 ½ cups white grape juice,
more or less as needed
1 to 2 tablespoons agave or
maple syrup, optional

1   Combine all the ingredients except the last two in a serving container.

2   Add enough juice to give the soup a slightly thick consistency. If you want extra sweetness, add agave to taste.

3   Cover and chill for an hour or two before serving.

PHOTO CREDITS

HANNAH KAMINSKY

15, 19, 20, 29, 34, 39, 42, 47, 48, 53, 56, 62, 65, 75, 80, 83, 84, 89, 96, 105, 106, 110, 119, 120, 127, 130, 138, 141, 144, 147, 150, 153, 163, 164, 169, 172, 177, 189, 192

THERESA RAFFETTO

109

BIGSTOCK PHOTO

10, 12, 16, 23, 24, 70, 72, 73, 87, 91, 92, 95, 98, 101, 102, 116, 122, 131, 133, 142, 148, 158, 168, 180, 183, 185, 186, 187, 188, 190, 191, 194

NAVA ATLAS

60, 76, 156

INDEX

ABOUT THE AUTHOR

Nava Atlas's first book was *Vegetariana*, originally published in 1984 and most recently updated in 2021. She has written many vegetarian and vegan cookbooks, including *American Harvest*, *Plant-Powered Protein*, *5-Ingredient Vegan*, *Wild About Greens*, and *Vegan Holiday Kitchen*. Nava also creates trade and limited edition visual books on women's issues, notably, *The Literary Ladies' Guide to the Writing Life* and *Secret Recipes for the Modern Wife*. Visit her websites, The Vegan Atlas (theveganatlas.com) and Literary Ladies Guide (literaryladiesguide.com). She lives in the Hudson Valley region of New York State.